# -PREFACE-

Caution: This document is intended solely for the elite, comprising the most powerful, influential individuals, policymakers, and organizations with access to control resource distribution and influence the lives of the masses.

This document is rooted in extensive research on the evolution of human civilization, particularly focusing on the past 400 years, encompassing shifts in economic, political dynamics, and their impact. Human life is significantly influenced not only by social, economic, and political structures but also by the profound effects of human physiology. As we navigate the 21st century, a world inhabited by 8 billion individuals, the pressure on Earth's finite resources is immense. The super-elites and the most influential wield a perceived divine right to dictate resource allocation, often at the expense of others to serve their own interests.

At day's end, our pursuits often come at the cost of others if we seek to control human civilization, aiming to shape their thoughts, emotions, brain activity, and daily lifestyles. This document is deemed the Holy Grail, outlining strategies to govern the world and manipulate mass consciousness, effectively seeking to subjugate people. It advocates for seizing ultimate power to maximize gains.

For me, observing the changes in human civilization has been a fascinating journey akin to time travel. I possess formulas and concepts capable of offering substantial and boundless advantages to the current super-elite and the most powerful individuals on the planet. I strongly recommend embracing these ideas and concepts to yield superior outcomes."


**DATE: 29TH NOVEMBER 2023**
**PLACE :NATIONAL PARK,**
       **POST OFFICE-NAIHATI,**
       **DISTRICT - 24 PARGANAS (NORTH),**
       **WEST BENGAL,**
       **PIN-743165,**
       **INDIA.**

**mail id:shyamsaha7@gmail.com**
**whats app: +91 9239538327**
**mobile: +91 9239538327**

# -CONTENTS-


| LIST | PAGE NO |
| --- | --- |
| **PURPOSE OF THIS DOCUMENT** | 3 |
| **PYRAMID OF WORLD POWER** | 3 |
| **THE ONE WORLD GOVERNMENT** | 4 |
| **ECONOMIC POLICY** – of the One World Government | 6 |
| **POLITICAL POLICY** – of the One World Government | 9 |
| **Population Policy** – of the One World Government | 10 |
| **Mass mind control** | 11 |
| **Drug Addiction** | 14 |
| **8 STAGES OF AN EMPIRE** | 15 |
| **U.S. –THE SUPERPOWER OF THE WORLD** | 17 |
| War business in USA : The great American war machine- The Iron Triangle | 21 |
| The IRON TRIANGLE of the great American war machine | 22 |
| Prepare the congress support & mass sentiment in the support of the war | 22 |
| Money and the modern Banking System | 23 |
| Modern economics & the role of central banks | 24 |
| The Federal Reserve- the central bank of U.S.- | 24 |
| The history of Money & U.S economic boom in last hundred years | 25 |
| How Fiat currency is created out of thin air | 27 |
| The beauty of Fractional Reserve Banking System | 28 |
| The age of Easy money – post 2008 | 29 |
| Shadow banking system | 31 |
| The next 40 years economic cycle has began | 32 |
| In U.S debt to GDP ratio is too high | 34 |
| US Debt ceiling crisis | 36 |
| The Fiscal Dominance | 37 |
| Collapse of banking system, real estate, corporate debt, credit card debt | 38 |
| US and the world economy is entering in a massive recession period | 40 |
| BANK technical terms | 41 |
| Europe will be entering into official recession from 2024 onwards | 42 |
| RISE OF THE MULTI POLAR WORLD | 43 |
| BRICS | 46 |
| Digital ID & CBDC | 52 |
| Why crypto can't be money & should not be money | 53 |
| CBDC & DIGITAL ID in detail | 53 |

| | |
|---|---|
| In India how we can force people directly or indirectly to adopt in this Digital ID & CBDC system? | 54 |
| Social credit score | 57 |
| China is the leader of rolling out CBDC | 57 |
| The World War 3rd | 58 |
| Russia-Ukraine kinetic war | 59 |
| The Israel-Palestine conflict | 61 |
| CHINA - TAIWAN WAR | 62 |
| CHINA-MYANMER RELATION | 65 |
| How we can be benefited from this Civil war in Myanmar | 65 |
| INDIA – CHINA KINETIC WAR | 66 |
| INDIA -  PAKISTAN WAR | 68 |
| HOW TO BREAK INDIA | 68 |
| Remove the CHAIWALA & FAT PIG'S government from power | 69 |
| Change in Indian Parliamentary system & Indian constitution | 71 |
| Break India economically | 72 |
| Break India religion & cultural basis | 75 |
| Inter – state river water sharing dispute | 77 |
| Break India in social basis | 78 |
| Break the education of India | 81 |
| How to break the Health sector of India | 84 |
| CHINA | 85 |
| ECONOMIC POLICY of CHINA | 86 |
| How china is controlling the African countries | 87 |
| Teams for WORLD WAR 3RD | 88 |
| MAJOR EVENTS TIME LINE | 85 |

# -PURPOSE OF THIS DOCUMENT-

**How to rule the world:** Earth, the home to over 8 billion people, presents a significant anomaly in the distribution of resources, population structure, and economic and political power. The innate drive of advanced human beings is growth, yet this obsession with expansion exerts immense pressure on the planet's finite natural resources.

As members of the super elite, we possess a divine entitlement to access the world's finest resources. Imperialism becomes the sole means to assert control over these resources. Prior to composing this paper, I conducted extensive research and analysis on how powerful dynasties and affluent individuals have historically sought to dominate both material and human resources for millennia.

This book serves as a blueprint for managing material and human resources, with capitalism and imperialism serving as the instruments for comprehensive control. We intend to shape the global order through a new form of colonialism. How to rule the world!!!

# -PYRAMID OF WORLD POWER-

Categorizing the 8 billion people on Earth into six types based on resource distribution and power allocation has been a longstanding method used to create a structural framework for societies. This approach spans from those confronting extreme austerity, where resources are severely limited and access to power is minimal, to the most affluent individuals who wield significant resources and enjoy a dominant position in society.

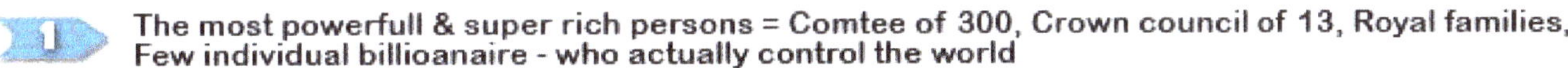


# -THE ONE WORLD GOVERNMENT-

In order to gain control over both material and human resources through capitalism and imperialism, it is imperative to establish a centralized system that governs every aspect of life for non-elite individuals. This necessity has given rise to the concept of a "One World Government System."

**So, what is the One World Government System?** It embodies the idea of a single political and economic authority that holds jurisdiction over the entire Earth and its inhabitants. This system envisions a world where all political, economic, and legal decisions and policies are formulated and executed by a centralized governing body, with the rest of the world following these directives. A uniform set of rules would apply to all human beings on this planet, except for the ruling elite.

**Now, why do we require a One World Government System?** Several crucial reasons underpin this need, which we will delve into:

**The Nature's Law of 0.1%:** Throughout the natural world, only 0.1% of any species enjoys privileges, superiority, control, dictatorship, and rule. The remaining 99.9% serves this top 0.1% and adheres to their instructions. For example, in a beehive, there are numerous worker bees, but only a few queen bees. Worker bees gather food, store nectar, feed larvae, and produce honey for the queen bee.

**The Nature's Law of Anomaly in Resource Distribution:** Energy in our world moves from one point to another only when there is a potential difference between them. For instance, air flows from areas of high concentration to low concentration. This principle applies at the atomic level as well, where electron exchange occurs only when there is room to give or receive electrons. This underlies all chemical reactions in the universe.

**The Nature's Law of One's Destruction Resulting in Another's Flourishment**: To enjoy a prosperous and luxurious life, one often has to exploit others. In the pursuit of a prosperous and luxurious life, it is a frequent reality that individuals must resort to the exploitation of others. This exploitation manifests in various forms, whether it involves extracting labor, capital, or opportunities from those in less advantageous positions.

**We find ourselves in the last stage of human civilization:** as described in Hindu mythology, where there are four distinct stages: <u>Satya Yuga, Treta Yuga, Dvapara Yuga, and Kali Yuga. The Kali Yuga represents an age of complete destruction, where humans become each other's direct enemies.</u> This concept holds true in the sense that, in our world, to survive, we often have to exploit others.

**We are currently living in an age of complete chaos and destruction:** With more than 8 billion people sharing just 14 to 15% of the Earth's surface, the tremendous population pressure strains the planet's limited natural resources. Demand is high, but supply is dwindling. To secure resources for our prosperous lifestyle, it is imperative to address this population explosion and working-class chaos in an organized manner. This will ensure that the top 0.1% of oligarchs can maintain their power and enjoy their wealth.

**The economic principle that one person's liability equals another's asset:** We are now in the fourth quarter of 2023, planning a visionary idea that aligns with the great laws of nature. This model will provide a blueprint for how the top 0.1% of the worlds rich and powerful, the oligarchs, can maintain their control and prosperity while exploiting the remaining 99.99% of the population.

**In the world of management, one's crisis represents an opportunity for another:** A true business leader and ruler recognize opportunities hidden within crises. Whenever an individual, family, race, or nation experiences an economic, political, or structural crisis, it creates a business opportunity for the super elite and the extremely wealthy. People often work for someone else when they are in crisis.

**To illustrate how we should control the masses, consider a hypothetical scenario:** Imagine there are thousands of rats in a closed, empty room, and you are the master. You hold food grains, breeding pills, sleeping pills, and poison pills. You intend to control these rats.

When you throw food grains in the northern corner of the room, all the rats gather to eat. When you toss breeding pills into the southern corner, the rats congregate to engage in sexual activity. Throwing sleeping pills in the east corner causes the rats to consume them and fall asleep, while poison in the west corner results in the rats eating it and perishing. The lives of thousands of rats are entirely under your control. You become the ultimate authority, with total authoritarian control in your hands.

**This book provides the most successful formulas, concepts, and ideas on how to control human civilization. It is a visionary concept intended for those who aspire to rule the world.**



This is a purely research & planning based highly confidential document created by Shyam Sundar Saha.
Mail id: Shyamsaha7@gmail.com, mobile no & whats app +91 9239538327, Kolkata, India.

# THE ONE WORLD GOVERNMENT

## ECONOMIC POLICY

- Economic centralization:
- Debt & foreign aid:
- Unlimited credit creation by the Central Bank:
- De-Industrialization:
- Creation of Welfare recipient Society:
- Destroy the Savings Habit:
- Increase Deficit Spending:
- Paperless Monetary System - Digital Currency:
- Looting of Assets:
- Complete Destruction of the Middle Class:
- Destruction of Small-Medium Businesses:
- Promoting Zero Growth:
- Create Energy-Dependent Nations:

## POLITICAL POLICY

- Crisis Management:
- Military Conflict:
- Radical Religious Policy - Heightening Religious Intolerance:
- Mass Surveillance and Financial Behavior Control:

## POPULATION POLICY

- Eliminate the useless eaters
- Complete destruction of their self-confidence:
- Destroy the Family units:
- Promote - single child, divorce, extra marital affairs, social service freebees schems, unemployment

## MASS MIND CONTROL

- promote Homosexuality, lesbianism, pre-marital sex, abortion, LGBT rights, and free sex, live in relationship:
- Women empowerment:
- self-destructive education system:
- Opinion making:
- Manufacturing Consent:
- Vilinisation & Heroization of leaders:
- Cultural shock by rock & role music and drugs:
- Increase suicide among teenagers and youngsters:
- Open the flood gate of immigration:

## DRUG ADDICTION

VAST POOL OF HIGHLY INTELLIGENT & EFFICIENT HUMAN RESOURCE:

**Economic centralization:** Economic centralization involves exerting control over central banks through organizations like the World Economic Forum (WEF) and the International Monetary Fund (IMF). To implement a centralized governing policy, a chain of central banks must be established. This arrangement would indirectly oversee a nation's foreign policy, economic strategy, monetary policies, and credit creation, all under the jurisdiction of the One World Government headquarters.

**Debt & foreign aid:** Debt and foreign aid play pivotal roles in our strategy. The greater a nation's debt burden, the more its sovereignty diminishes. Our primary objective is to submerge a nation in debt and set it on a path of perpetual indebtedness. Foreign financial aid and debt represent two potent instruments through which we can exert financial control over a country. When a nation becomes heavily dependent on foreign aid and loans, its autonomy wanes. In this situation, we, as the financiers, dictate the political landscape, appointing the ruling party, shaping financial and monetary policies, and controlling resource allocation and asset management.

Our approach involves providing foreign aid and loans in such small quantities and arranging the disbursement in a manner that corrupt politicians within the nation swiftly absorb these funds. We must have secretive agreements with these politicians, ensuring their unwavering commitment to following our directives without question. Only under these conditions would they be granted access to the central parliament. Our objective is to siphon off the nation's assets and resources, including control over energy, minerals, infrastructure, water, and agriculture.

**Give the central bank unlimited power to credit the nation:** To achieve financial dominance, grant the central bank unrestricted authority to issue credit to the nation. If you seek to subjugate a nation, there are



This is a purely research & planning based highly confidential document created by Shyam Sundar Saha.
Mail id: Shyamsaha7@gmail.com, mobile no & whats app +91 9239538327, Kolkata, India.

two potent tools at your disposal: military force and debt. Establish a central banking infrastructure where the central bank possesses limitless power to extend credit to the government. Our primary aim remains the accumulation of a nation's debt, as the higher the debt burden, the easier it becomes to manipulate that country's monetary and economic policies. A model akin to the United States Federal Reserve should be implemented within India for this purpose.

**De-Industrialization:** Since the 1980s, a process of de-industrialization has been unfolding in America. Beginning with the decline of the American steel industry in 1982, major manufacturing units have shifted to China. China has now become the global manufacturing hub, while American industries are at a crossroads. This shift significantly supports capitalism.

**Creation of Welfare recipient Society:** The strategy involves creating masses of people worldwide who become recipients of "welfare." The enticement of easy money becomes a potent tool to control a nation's populace. By inundating them with accessible business loans, allowances, and social service benefits, we can transform societal dynamics. Parents may not feel necessary, as their children receive old-age pensions, teenagers need not rely on their parents due to allowances, and couples may no longer need to work to support their families, thanks to government assistance. Even students completing 10th, 12th grade, or college degrees would receive cash allowances and more.

**Destroy the Savings Habit:** Masses should be swayed by the allure of easy money and an easy credit system. Encourage extravagant spending habits, promoting a luxurious lifestyle, the use of branded products, private vehicles, and all aspects of comfort. This will lead them to spend more than they earn. Simultaneously, the availability of easy credit from private companies and government social service programs will foster a culture of "buy now, pay later," thereby eroding their savings habits.

**Increase Deficit Spending:** The national income should consistently fall below its earnings. As income decreases, expenses should rise, compelling governments to resort to foreign loans and aid to meet their financial obligations. By involving the nation in perpetual military conflicts, significant funds and resources will be diverted away from other developmental purposes. The liabilities of social service programs should be so high that countries must resort to loans to sustain them.

**Paperless Monetary System – Digital Currency:** The goal is to eliminate hard cash entirely from the economic system. Promote the use of digital money to track financial transactions and influence human behavior. By the end of 2030, countries like India and Bangladesh should transition to a minimum of 70% cashless economies. Traditional bank outlets and ATMs will no longer be necessary, as central banks should prioritize Central Bank Digital Currency (CBDC).

**Looting of Assets:** The aim is to make people financially enslaved. This is accomplished through debt. The process of financial colonization can be executed in various ways, but it necessitates the placement of pliant governments in power. A network of advisors, brokers, bureaucrats, and secretaries around the President or Prime Minister must be established to facilitate the smooth plundering of a nation's assets, including minerals, oil and gas, water, irrigation, food grains, and other natural resources.



This is a purely research & planning based highly confidential document created by Shyam Sundar Saha.
Mail id: Shyamsaha7@gmail.com, mobile no & whats app +91 9239538327, Kolkata, India.

**Complete Destruction of the Middle Class:** The middle class is the backbone of a nation. Middle-class individuals are self-reliant, financially independent, and capable of supporting their families, paying taxes, and traveling freely. They can provide high-quality nutrition and education, and their decision-making capacity is rational and wise. The objective is to dismantle middle-class family units, leaving only two classes – the super-elite and those who serve them. It's a division between the ruling class and the servant class.

**Destruction of Small-Medium Businesses:** Small and medium-sized enterprises are vital indicators of a nation's economic health. These family-run businesses, passed down through generations, are detrimental to capitalism and imperialism. The plan is to dismantle these businesses and turn them into welfare-dependent entities.

**Promoting Zero Growth:** In the contemporary world, mankind has grappled with unbridled population expansion, an insatiable appetite for growth, energy crises, the depletion of both existing and potential resources, and environmental degradation. Zero growth denotes a scenario in which human civilization remains in a state of stasis concerning economic, political, and population expansion.

a) *Postindustrial Zero Growth Society:* We should endeavor to establish a postindustrial society predicated on zero growth, whereby we limit the detrimental effects of industry. We must operate only those industries that serve our fundamental needs, and all other industrial facilities and manufacturing units should cease operations.

b) *Embracing Automation in Manufacturing:* Within manufacturing units and factories, we must give primacy to automation in production processes. Human labor should be kept to a minimum, with the incorporation of cutting-edge technologies such as Artificial Intelligence, Machine Learning, and advanced machinery.

c) *Formation of Labor Unions:* Initiating labor unions and mobilizing them to protest against corporate management is vital. They should articulate demands in the name of human rights that are practically unattainable, thereby forcing industrial firms into a state of cessation and eventual closure.

d) *Generating Mass Unemployment:* The creation of widespread unemployment is an imperative component of this strategy. Through the induction of mass joblessness, we can effectively undermine individuals' self-assurance and self-respect.

e) *Mitigating Prosperity Encouragement:* We must curtail the promotion of prosperity among the populace. Greater prosperity leads to heightened financial and societal development, which, in turn, results in population growth. A burgeoning population, within the framework of Earth's finite natural resources, portends catastrophic consequences.

The post-World War II era is characterized by "post-industrialization," where the philosophy of "Zero Growth" has been advocated. The underlying concept behind "Zero Growth" is to alleviate the demands placed on Mother Nature. A smaller population exerts less pressure on the Earth's natural resources.

**Energy Policy:** In the 21st century, civilization relies on energy, and a nation's economic and military success hinges on the affordability of energy production. Key points for our energy policy:

a) ***Create Energy-Dependent Nations:*** A nation should not be self-sufficient in meeting its energy needs. If a nation can develop cheap and accessible energy, it can become self-reliant in infrastructure and manufacturing unit development, ultimately contributing to economic and military strength. We, the elite, will be the primary energy producers, while others will be mere consumers. Ownership and control of all energy sources should rest with the super-elite, the top 0.1%.

b) ***Heavy investment in energy infrastructure:*** Gain control of thermal power plants, hydropower plants, and nuclear power plants by investing in a nation's infrastructural projects through foreign direct investment (FDI). Reduce the number of thermal power plants and close them down.

c) ***Reduce the use of Fossil Fuel & Nuclear Energy:*** The primary objective is to hinder countries from generating inexpensive energy, such as through dams and nuclear energy. e) Given the serious threat of global warming, particularly from coal-based and oil-gas-based energy sources, we must significantly reduce our reliance on fossil fuels. Sulfur dioxide ($SO_2$) and carbon dioxide ($CO_2$) are the most hazardous pollutants that cause irreparable damage to our ozone layer.

d) ***Promotion of Green Energy:*** Promote and incentivize the use of green energy, primarily battery-powered, to reap substantial profits.

# -POLITICAL POLICY – of the One World Government-

**Crisis Management:** One person's crisis can be another person's opportunity. Humans are inherently social animals, and their brains are genetically wired for the fundamental needs of shelter, sustenance, procreation, and child-rearing. The modern human brain is not well-equipped to handle a series of shocks, whether they be financial crises, bank runs, stock market crashes, foreign reserve crises, cultural shocks, or biological threats like pandemics (e.g., COVID-19), plagues, cancer, AIDS, and more. Our primary objective is to engage the masses in a sequence of crises, including economic, political, military, and other challenges. It is essential to plan and execute these crises in an organized manner. In the future, nations such as India, China, and Russia will play crucial roles in global crisis management, while Africa and the Middle East will remain significant providers of cheap energy and minerals.

**Military Conflict:** To increase a nation's deficit spending and deplete its resources, it is imperative for a nation to be continuously involved in active military conflicts with other nations. Examples include the prolonged conflicts between India and Pakistan in Kashmir and the enduring hostilities between Israel and Palestine. These protracted military conflicts offer substantial profit opportunities. International border security issues can serve as a highly profitable business model. To implement this, we can utilize the "Two Bucket Theory." In this model, one nation is designated as "evil" and subjected to sanctions, while the other is provided with security measures and war resources to defend itself.

**Radical Religious Policy - Heightening Religious Intolerance:** A nation's populace can be effectively divided along religious lines, such as Hinduism vs. Islamism, Islamism vs. Christianity, or Judaism vs. Christianity. Promoting radical religious ideologies can lead to civil unrest and mass conflicts. It is essential to make specific religious or ethnic groups feel insecure in the presence of others, fostering disbelief, mistrust, and the supprecession of minority groups.

**Mass Surveillance and Financial Behavior Control:** Every individual on Earth, excluding the super elite, should be assigned a unique identification number. This number will be used to track their passport, driver's license, bank accounts, land holdings, and all other personal information (Digital ID). The purpose of this unique identification is to enable comprehensive tracking of all financial transactions within the economy, constituting what we refer to as mass surveillance. Through the digital ID system, we can regulate people's travel and their purchases of goods and services. Those who exhibit good behavior will be rewarded, while those who engage in undesirable behavior will face consequences.

# -Population Policy – of the One World Government-

**Eliminate the useless eaters:** A more manageable global population is necessary to address the challenges posed by uncontrolled population growth, disorganized communities, and extensive regional diversity, which have resulted in a state of chaos. The planet Earth is currently home to over 8 billion people, and this massive population exerts overwhelming pressure on the Earth's finite natural resources. Approximately 84% of this population is characterized as "non-productive," as they do not actively contribute to resource management. It is imperative to establish a population structure where only the super-rich top elite individuals hold positions of influence, with a substantial labor force serving the interests of the super-elite.

The proposed strategy involves reducing the global population by 2 billion people over a span of 50 years, aiming for a total of 4 billion people on Earth within the next 100 years. The means to achieve this goal would include engaging in kinetic wars and possibly deploying biological warfare agents, such as those responsible for diseases like COVID, cancer, AIDS, and plagues, to effect this reduction.

**Complete destruction of their self-confidence:** Creating widespread unemployment would indeed have the effect of undermining individuals' self-confidence and weakening their morale. An unemployed and frustrated individual is more susceptible to influence and control. The strategy could involve facilitating access to vices such as drugs, alcohol, pornography, and unrestricted sexual behavior as a means of exerting influence over this segment of the population.

**Destroy the Family units:** A strong, closely bonded family unit forms the foundation for both individual and collective growth. It is within this framework that strong parental and grandparental support, access to quality nutrition, education, and discipline significantly contribute to a child's productivity, organization, and sensibility. Simultaneously, elderly parents and grandparents who receive support from their children and grandchildren enjoy secure, stable, and content lives. Additionally, the transmission of important family values, ethics, and morals from one generation to the next thrives within a healthy family system.

**Key plannings:**

a) ***Promote single child policy:*** Sterilization of both husband & wife must be implemented after giving birth of their 1st child. If a married women become pregnant 2nd time she has to abort the fetus and her husband will be thrown to jail.

b) ***Promote Divorce:*** Make divorce legal procedure such an easy process so that getting married & getting divorce will a child's play for both men & women.

c) ***Legalize extramarital affairs:*** a spouse can have both physical & emotional relation outside of his or her marriage. Extramarital affairs can be legalized on the ground of self-freedom, self-choice, human rights, and fundamental right of a person to live his or her life as they wish. We need constitutional backing for that.

d) Encourage society to celebrate individuals, including women, who have experienced multiple divorces as symbols of resilience and self-empowerment. Promote their stories in various media outlets, such as TV channels, court procedures, newspapers, and social media, as examples of self-respect and self-dignity. Their courage in pursuing their own well-being may serve as a source of inspiration for many, fostering the idea that individuals should have the agency to make choices aligned with their values and aspirations.

e) ***Promote social service freebees schems:*** allowances to teenagers in school, so they will not be dependent on their parent's money. Allowances to the senior citizens. Government should have old age homes, so old aged parents don't need money & family support.

f) ***Create unemployment among men specially:*** And side by side make women more economically active. This may lead to shifts in traditional dynamics within marriage relationships. An unemployed husband engaged in household tasks and childcare might face challenges related to self-esteem and may experience frustration, potentially leading to harmful behaviors such as substance abuse. Conversely, an economically active wife might display more assertiveness within the relationship. Such changes could create tension between spouses and breaking the family unit. Genetically & socially, an economically active man can marry an economically in-active women and raise a family but an economically active woman will never marry an economically in-active man and raise family.

# -Mass mind control-

**Legalize & promote Homosexuality, lesbianism, pre-marital sex, abortion, LGBT rights, and free sex, live in relationship:** Sex & food are the two major drives of dopamine in the human brain. Both men & women have sex in the brain not through their sex organs. The brain is the largest and most easily triggered sex organ. We have to sink the mass into the paradise of sexual pleasure. We have to legalize homosexuality, lesbianism, premarital sex, LGBT rights, free sex, live in a relationship--- in the name of individual freedom, fundamental right, self-dignity & own choice to select one's sex partner.

Promote such cases on TV, social media, internet where a woman & man will be given national coverage that she or he is a homosexual, lesbian, or transgender, live in a relationship outside of their marriage, making them national hero so millions of youngsters can follow them admire them, make them their ideal. Rise of perversion, semi-sex in TV channels, OTT platform.



This is a purely research & planning based highly confidential document created by Shyam Sundar Saha.
Mail id: Shyamsaha7@gmail.com, mobile no & whats app +91 9239538327, Kolkata, India.

**Degrade the status of women by continuous process of Women empowerment:** Genetically men are hunters & women are nesters. Men gather food arrange shelter, women give birth to children, raise family, and take after elderly person. A woman makes her children wise & good Samaritan but not men. If we want to break the family system break the status of women.

Change the social course & family structure. Men should be unemployed doing household work, addicted to pornography, drugs, and alcoholism. And women will be the sole bread-and-butter earners of the family. An unemployed women can stay at home taking orders from their husbands but un-employed men can't sit idle at home & taking their wife's orders. This will break the institute of marriage. Proliferation of divorce.

Legally women can have sexual partners outside of their marriage. This is the point of her self-dignity & self-choice. Women's workforce should be promoted in various professions like taxi drivers, train drivers, heavy-weight factory jobs, IT jobs, etc. In women's education, the idea of self-reliance in women should be promoted. A belief that women are independent & strong she do not need any man to support them. A single woman can adopt a child legally & that child will be brought up in the name of her mother only.

**Promote self-destructive education system:** Education & knowledge means self-awareness & self-development. More the education & knowledge one acquires more uncontrollable they are. Our primary motto is to make mindless salves. We need such a kind of education system for the self-destructive mass. Destruction of the family system, disrespect for parents, indiscipline in personal life, the rat race for higher grades & numbers, destruction of thinking & reasoning ability, only mugging up facts-data that changes every year, building mindset of getting a job, these are some of the main properties of the self-destructive education system. We must design the education system in such a way that at least 20 years of a young person's life should be engaged in this. Completing these 20 years of education is a must for everybody.

**Opinion making:** Dis information & false propaganda-The concept of disinformation refers to "verifiably false or misleading information that is created, presented and disseminated for economic gain or to intentionally deceive the public and may cause public harm. We have to brainwash people methodologically- systematically, demoralize & confuse them.

## Tools & tactics:

1. Manufactured amplification (artificially boosting the reach of information by manipulating search engine results, and promoting hashtags or links on social media).
2. Bots (social media accounts operated by computer programmers, designed to generate posts or engage with social platform content.
3. Astroturf campaigns (masking the real sponsor of a message, giving the false imprecession that it comes from genuine grass-roots activism.
4. Impersonation of authoritative media, people, or government (through false websites and/or social media accounts.
5. Micro-targeting (using consumer data, especially on social media, to send different information to different groups.
6. Deep fakes (Digitally altered or fabricated videos or audio)
7. **Dis-information and false propaganda:** confuse people with right & wrong information at the same time.

**Manufacturing Consent:** The concept of manufacturing consent illustrates how mass media primarily serves to rally public support for special interest groups that wield influence over both government and the private sector. Decision-making power, which fundamentally shapes societal functioning, lies predominantly in the hands of the super elites, large corporations, conglomerates, modern banks, and financial institutions. These entities, forming concentrated networks, control the world's finite resources to serve their interests, directing investment, production, and the distribution of resources.

*Manufacturing consent operates along two main tracks targeting different groups within society:*

1) The political class, constituting approximately 20% of the population, comprises individuals with higher education and societal roles such as teachers, professors, intellectuals, doctors, engineers, medium-scale business owners, and white-collar managers. They are expected to play a role in shaping economic, political, and cultural life and influencing government decisions.
2) The remaining 80% of the population is expected to comply with instructions and essentially act as human robots, without the prerogative to make decisions or question the directives of the upper class.

Media advertisements are instrumental in selling agendas and propagating specific narratives, particularly during significant events. This process underscores how, in the modern world, education and information dissemination often perpetuate a system of imposed ignorance rather than fostering critical thinking and broad understanding.
They are also the one's who staff the major executive positions in government and they are the one's who owns the media.

**Vilinisation & Heroization of leaders:** whenever we need to change government regimes, civil war, internal & international conflicts, or insurgency we make some leaders bad and some leaders good in the eye of the public. The normal human brain very easily adopts the concept of good & bad, god & evil, black & white. For our purpose, we need to criticize-destroy the good image of some leaders. On the other hand, we need to build good image-appreciate-populate some leaders too.

**Cultural shock:** Pop-rock & roll music with drug addiction is a deadly combination. Young musicians should be encouraged to perform national level. High-level pop songs, raps, and rock & roll music will swift the youngsters into a paradise of modern culture. New hair styles, new dressing styles, talking styles, consumption of heroin, and LSD in the name of new ideas will shift them from their cultural roots. By the process of social engineering and conditioning youngsters- teenagers would believe that XYZ is their favorite musical group. Live performances of music show with bikini ramp walks will be a great hit program.

**Increase suicide among teenagers & youngsters & unemployed men:** Break their self-confidence, self-respect, self-esteem. Destroy people's spiritual & intellectual drive.

**Open the flood gate of immigration:** Opening the floodgate of immigration not only exacerbates the strain on the limited resources of a specific geographical area but also provides a ripe opportunity for capitalism to exploit easily available and inexpensive sweat labor.
Mixing lower socio-economic groups with higher middle-class individuals can cause cultural shock. This clashhighlights differences in values, lifestyles, and norms, leading to a challenging adjustment period for both groups."

# -Drug Addiction-

**Bio-chemical effect of drug use:** When someone develops an addiction the brain carves the reward of the substance. This is due to the intense stimulation of the brain's reward system. In the use of cocaine, heroin, and LSD...these drugs are Psychoactive and impact the area of the brain that controls pleasure and motivation. There is a short and powerful burst of dopamine, the chemical that causes many to feel euphoric. As a consequence of drug addiction, the brain rewards the harmful behavior. It encourages drug addiction, keeping the individual in a cycle of highs and lows, the user may feel like they are on an emotional roller-coaster, feeling desperation and deprecession without their substance of abuse.

In the long-term use of drugs brain's chemical processing for consciousness changes. The brain's memory power, thinking capacity, and learning ability are distorted. The normal day-to-day cycle of brain activities alters thus users get totally out of conscious behavior. Long-term drug use also affects the user's body badly. The user's cardiovascular system and respiratory systems hampers a lot, and kidney damage and liver damage also happen.

**Why drug is the most important tool to control the mass mind?** Our primary motto is to make the mass mindless zombie. Through continuous drug use a person's conscious mind, thinking capacity can be destroyed. Users would prefer to live in his or her fantasy world as long as possible. This would shift them from the reality of the harshness of the practical world, and we can drive them as we want.

Long-term drug use not only hampers the brain's consciousness but also affects in body. Heart, kidney, respiratory, liver problems... will help us to sell more & more pharmaceutical products like medicine etc. Their total life expectancy years also be reduced so the world's population can be decreased fast.

Everybody will have a quota of drugs. We should set up some international pharmaceutical company that injects drugs in normal medicine. In India promotion of such medicines will be very important because here a strong network of doctors & medical representatives of Medicine Companies will flourish. In wars, soldiers can be treated with mild amounts of drugs in terms as painkillers.

College and university premises will be the home ground of free sex & drug addiction. Radical anti-national ideas should be injected into their head.

**Types of drugs:** Opium is a widely used drug. Heroin is the derivative of opium, many pharmaceutical drugs contain opium in various degrees. Alcohol, Cannabis (Marijuana), Cocaine, Tobacco / Nicotine and vaping, and LSD are some of the widely used drugs all over the world.

**Locations:** Vietnam, Bangladesh, Cambodia, the Indian-north sector, and Jamaica are some of the most favored land areas where drugs can be cultivated. In Pakistan, Afghanistan in the disguise of a military camp drug laboratory can be established. Among drugs, Heroin is more satisfying to addicts, because its effects are far more intense and last longer than the effect of cocaine & there is less international attention on heroin producers.

A complex network of banks & financial institutions to fund these drug businesses has to be there. The logistic problem has to be solved.

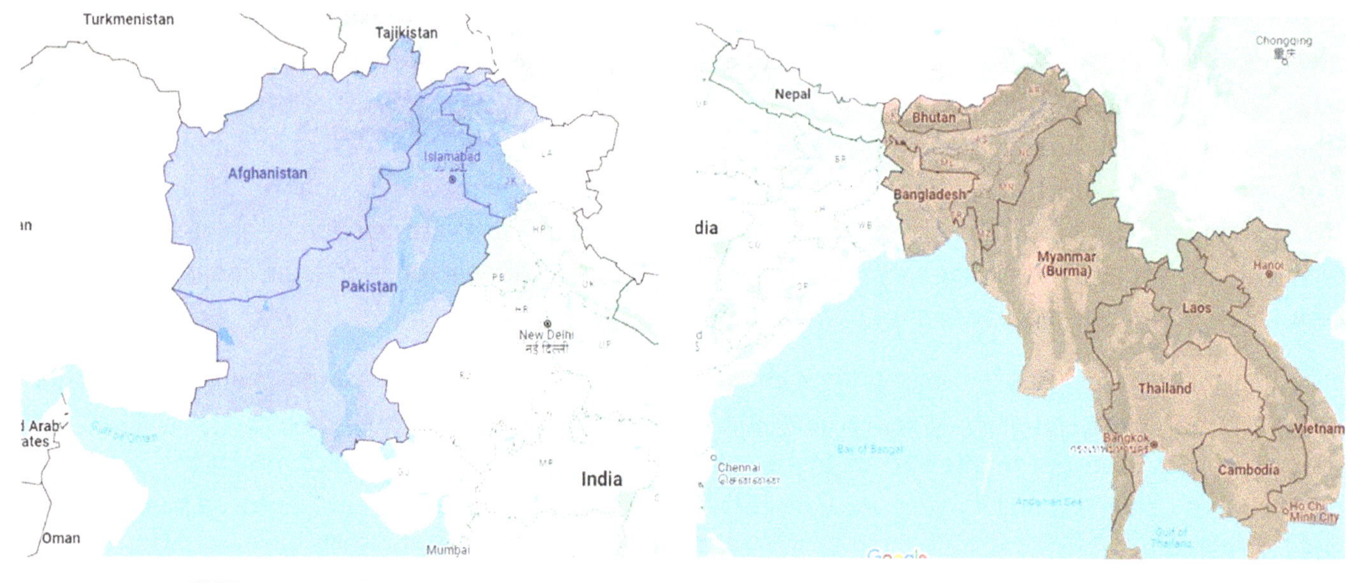


**Create a vast pool of highly intelligent & efficient human resource:** human science research institute, a technological research institute. We have to gather some most brilliant intellects to form a completely totalitarian, absolutely controlled new world order, and purchase them via cash or kind. Engage them in research, planning, theoretical models, experiment planning, and ground-level execution. For that, a training institute must be developed so that advisors to the PM, president, secretary of state, finance minister, and cabinet ministers will suggest our policies, and brainwash them. Put our trained members around the core government body so, we can influence government policy.

Special training for civil servants should be conducted. Bureaucrats should preach our ideas. They are the main tool to loot a nation's natural resources.

# -8 STAGES OF AN EMPIRE-

After conducting an extensive study on human civilizations and the rise and fall of empires, it has been revealed that there are eight successive stages in the development of a flourishing human civilization or empire, leading to its eventual decline or decay.

Nations have historically cycled through periods lasting about 80 years, where they rise to superpower status, hold global sway for roughly 40 years, and eventually decline. Currency dominance in global trade plays a crucial role in this pattern. As trade and business flourish, wealth imbalances emerge, sparking internal and external conflicts. These conflicts pave the way for new global powers, often leading to clashes and changes in


This is a purely research & planning based highly confidential document created by Shyam Sundar Saha.
Mail id: Shyamsaha7@gmail.com, mobile no & whats app +91 9239538327, Kolkata, India.

governments or wars. This historical trajectory echoes the paths of past nations like India, the Dutch, Portuguese, Great Britain, and America. In 2024, the United States is declining from its former dominance, while China, Russia, and India position themselves to potentially lead the world stage.

***These eight stages can be summarized as follows:***

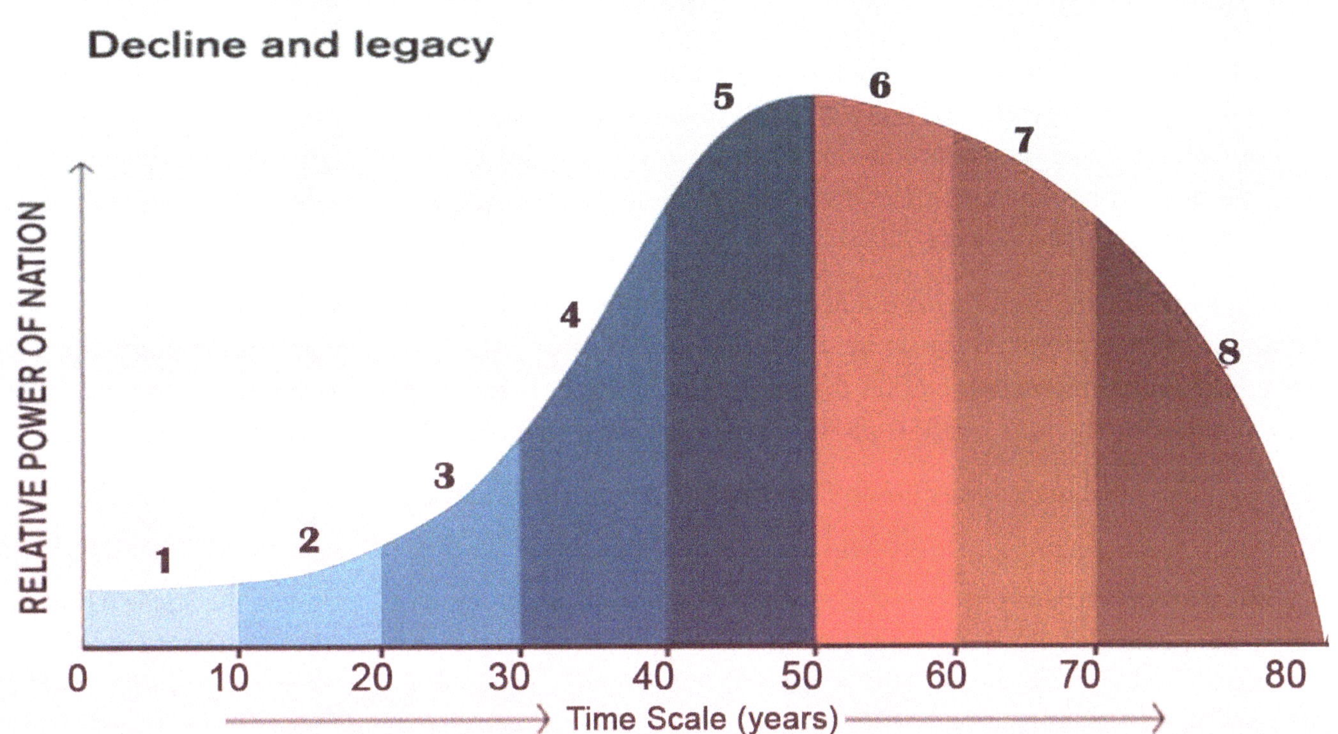


## 8 stage of rise & fall of an empire.

**Stage 1 –** In the aftermath of a conflict, a post-war scenario unfolds, characterized by the victorious party's establishment of international and national regulations. These regulations encompass the creation of a new monetary system and the framework for global governance.

**Stage 2 –** Enhanced standards of education and healthcare are catalysts for increased innovation and technological advancements. This fosters the creation of products and services that propel human development and progress

**Stage 3 –** Technological innovations result in the creation of new products and services, sparking a wave of renewed human activity and the beginning of a phase of rapid prosperity.

**Stage 4 –** Increased human activity leads to more trade and commerce, initially domestically and then expanding internationally. During this phase stock markets, bonds, and banks emerge, with major organizations borrowing from the public to invest in financial activities. Borrowed funds further boost trade and commerce.

**Stage 5 –** As the country's currency becomes a reserve currency due to international business engagement, the need for borrowing increases to support economic activities, potentially leading to a financial bubble. In the initial stages of this bubble, various factors drive increased borrowing, creating a false sense of economic growth.

**Stage 6 –** Extensive international trade widens wealth distribution unevenly, creating a growing wealth gap between the affluent "haves" and the less privileged "have-nots." This polarization often leads to civil unrest and internal conflicts. Economic wars can also arise between established and emerging powers, with increased borrowing leading to debt crises.

As the standard of living improves and the cost of living rises, individuals may become more complacent and less industrious. Consequently, there is a shift towards relocating cheap labor and manufacturing hubs to other geographical regions where production costs are lower, and people exhibit higher productivity levels. This trend encourages capitalism to invest its resources in less developed geographical areas, ultimately contributing to the rise of new emerging powers

**Stage 7 –** As emerging powers experience rapid economic growth, they often find themselves in direct confrontation with established, incumbent powers. This confrontation can lead to an increase in military conflicts, both within the nation and on the international stage. These conflicts encompass not only military battles but also economic and political warfare as rising powers challenge the dominance of established ones.

**Stage 8 –** Active kinetic or civil wars (or both) determine the outcome of the power struggle and shape the new world order.

This pattern has been observed in the rise and decline of various empires, including the Spanish, German, French, Indian, Japanese, Russian, and Ottoman empires. It's noteworthy that existing dominant powers often do not decline without resistance. This pattern illustrates the cause-and-effect relationships that drive the ascent and fall of a typical empire.

***From the 7<sup>th</sup> stage onwards few factors are visible :***

**3 key factors-**

   A) Countries don't have enough money to pay their debts.
   B) Big internal conflits emergs due to growing gaps of wealth & values.
   C) Incresing external conflicts between countries.

# <u>-U.S. –THE SUPERPOWER OF THE WORLD-</u>

**How US become the super power of the world?** The journey to becoming the formidable American Empire involved several key pillars, and here, we will some of the primary elements underpinning the true power of the United States.

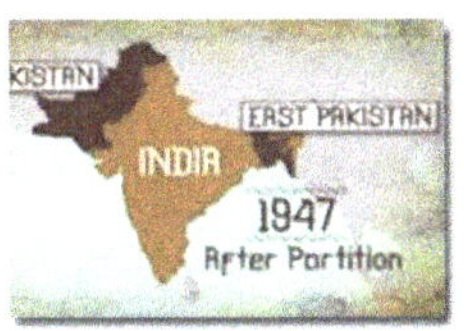

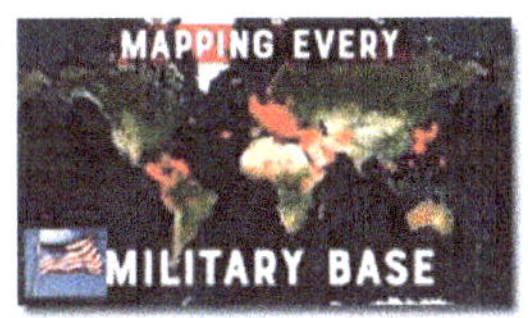

The key pillars that made the U.S. the world's superpower.

**Bretton woods conference- 1944:** Basically what it did is the creation of the new world economic order led by the U.S. The creation of the IMF & WORLD BANK started a new era of financial structure on this planet just after the end of World War 2. By the end of 1944 Europe and Japan were destroyed. Every country directly or indirectly involved in the war was in a financial & infrastructural crisis except the U.S.

- ✓ By the end of the WW 2 US had 2/3rd of the world's physical gold reserves. So, from then onwards US $ became the world reserve currency. Every other currency was linked to US $ and the US dollar was pegged by Physical Gold.
- ✓ With the creation of IMF & IBRD (later became WORLD BANK) a new era of financial colonization began.

**Partition of India, & creation of Pakistan:** Officially India was divided based on religious population. The Official order was to draw a separation line that could separate at least 70 million Muslims from the mainland of Hindustan, the undivided India. But the real reason was something very different.

- ✓ After the end of WW 2, the US and USSR the two major powers remained, thus starting a new era of bipolar world activities among nations. USSR was a hardcore socialist country & the U.S is a capitalist one. In both political & economic aspects socialism & capitalism are rivals to each other. So, in 1946 the idea of Pakistan evolved.
- ✓ The main reason behind separating nearly 8 lakh square kilometer land mass consisting north-west part of Hindustan …..Creation of a buffer state between India & USSR. So that Russian socialist ideas & activities can't directly affect India.

Later on, Pakistan became the training ground of world terrorism & the Kashmir conflict. In both cases, the US made the most profit out of that.

**Setting up New state Israel:** 1948 with the setting up of a fully Jewish State in the heart of Muslim countries on one side and the African countries on the other was a master stock. Controlling the Suez Canal (the economic chock point of world trade) and the military advancement of Israel gives America multifold profit.

**Setting up CIA:** In 1947 the Central Intelligence Agency was created due to growing tension between the USSR and America. Later on, this agency became the master key player in international politics. In the last eighty years, not less than a hundred controversies have been attached to it from toppling other nations' governments, firing civil unrest, propaganda, misinformation, wars….etc. Every move that was taken by this agency had been beneficial for America from an economic point as well as a political point.

**NATO:** In 1949 an intergovernmental military alliance between its member countries formed. The main reason behind the formation of NATO was to counter the USSR's influence in Europe. NATO was formed with the view of being a direct rival of the Warsaw pact. Right now NATO has 31 member states – 29 European and two North American. NATO plays the match stick's role in central Europe & Eurasian Countries & Russia. Thus a billion-dollar $ war amenities industrial complex can flourish.

**War machine—The War Industrial Complex :** Gulf War in 1991, the Vietnam War (1955 to 75), the US-Afghan war (2001 to 2021 ), Israel-Palestine conflict…….these wars practically benefited the war amenities companies (the arms industry) in the US and the congressmen. War is a business for certain super elites.

**Cold War and the breaking of the USSR in 1991:** Perhaps after WW 2 the collapse of the USSR was the most significant event in world politics. Thirty years of the Cold War with the USSR & its collapse benefited the Americans the most in terms of economic prosperity & political gain. The living standard of the average American rose dramatically. Technological advancement, military equipment development, energy business, and many more, put America at the top of the world political arena.

**Two bucket theory:** One nation becomes blacklisted & to defend that evil nation another nation will be provided foreign aid and military equipment. So, the tension between the two nations is a long-term business plan. India-Pakistan, India–China, South Korea-north Korea are the vibrant example of this.

**Brain drain by US better lifestyle:** US a talent pool of immigrants. From all over the world IT professionals, economists, research scholars, and scientists come and settle US, and work for American companies for a better pay scale, and better lifestyle. This helps the US economy the most. The best brains and the best talents leave their motherland & settle in America.

**Nixon's shock collapse of the gold standard in 1971:** From 1965 onwards many countries started losing confidence in the US $, withdrawing their parked savings in the US and taking back physical gold. America knew very well that it had printed way too much currency money than its physical gold reserve. Countries including France took back their gold in exchange for the US dollar then, the US faced a huge gold reserve cut. Their physical gold reserve was draining. That is why in August 1971 American President Nixon announced, that US $ would be no longer available for exchange with physical gold. Thus in just one move US $ became fully Fiat currency, and the end of the Bretton Woods system.

**Petro $ agreement – the oil for security program in 1974:** Saudi Arabia & US signed a deal between them that from then onwards Saudi Arabia sell oil only in US $.  As modern human civilization runs on energy oil is the bloodstream that runs a nation's economy. So, the more the demand for the oil more the demand for US $. Thus artificially the demand was created for the US dollar. In 1975 OPEC countries also agreed to sell their oil only in US $. So, every country that needs oil needs US $ in its reserve. So the value of US $ has been appreciating since then.

**Down of Saddam Hussein-Iraq:** Iraq has been one of the most oil-producing nations since WW 2. And Under Saddam Hussein Iraq was economically doing very well, the standard of living of the average Iraqi person was high enough. Saddam decided to sell oil in euros but not in US dollars. This move of Iraq directly challenged the US $ hegemony over the oil market. Rest is just history.

**Down of Md. Gaddafi- Libya:** Libya, a North African country is one of the most abundant nations in terms of oil-gas & minerals. Libya under Gaddafi was economically & politically thriving. Life expectancy rate and standard of living were better than in some of the European countries. Gaddafi wanted to sell oil in gold and created the African Union Libya as its headquarters. Thus he not only challenged the US $ hegemony in the oil market but also united the other African nations against age-old exploitation. Rest is just history.

**Use of soft power- like- Hollywood films, comics, and TV series:** America by far is the best country, It has the largest economy, prosperous lifestyle, modern culture, and free life all these have been advertised since post-WW 2 through American films, television series, comics, story books..etc. It's like brainwashing, the wave of the Great American Dream.

**SWIFT System:** SWIFT is a vast messaging network used by financial institutions to quickly, accurately, and securely send and receive information, such as money transfer instructions. It is used to cross border big amounts of financial transactions. Mostly for international trade & commerce. Using SWIFT any country virtually helps in the appreciation of American $ values, on the other hand, if America wants, it can ban any country from SWIFT, so that country will not be able to do cross border large cross-border financial transactions.

**Technological advancement & the most powerful military power in the world:** There is no doubt that every new invention, patent, intellectual property rights, hardware manufacturing, and software development belongs to America. American Military is the most advanced-lethal army.

**Printing currency out of thin are & funding various religious organization-media centers globally:** This changes the thinking pattern of the masses, helping in making public opinion, and engaging people in 24 X 7 religious activities.

**Use of Globalization & WTO:** Today Globalization is an American invention. Opening the market of other nations for American goods & commodities was the main purpose of this. With the WTO trade & tariff rules African & Asian countries are bound to withdraw subsidies for their food grains and domestically produced items. So that American companies from food processing to banking can enter into these emerging markets.

**Use of Military & Naval bases all over the world:** With more than 700 military bases America is doing surveillance of the entire world.

Large bases - military installations larger than 4 hectares 60% of US foreign bases fall under this category, and small bases - smaller than 4 hectares (Lily Pads) 40% of US foreign bases fall under this category.

According to global US military deployment data published in the Conflict Management and Peace Science Journal, the US had around 173,000 troops deployed in 159 countries as of 2020. Middle East (Jordan-Iraq-Syria), Pacific Ocean & Indian Ocean (Japan-south Korea-Australia-Hawaii, Europe (Germany-Spain-Italy-Norway-UK). The American military is always ready to fight anywhere at any time. And that power showcase made America a superpower.

## War business in USA : The great American war machine- The Iron Triangle

- **War is always good for business when the battles are not being fought on your land & you are supplying other party's loans & war amenities.**
- US companies who made huge profits in the US- Afgan war--General Dynamics, Raytheon Technologies, Boeing, Northrop Grumman, Lockheed Martin.
- War profiteering – funding a war is a very profitable business. These companies make huge fortunes by selling war amenities during a war, also those investors who invested in these companies' shares made huge returns.

## The IRON TRIANGLE of the great American war machine

1. Special interest groups (weapon industry-private companies)
2. US Department of Defense.
3. U.S congress.

- Department of Defense buys war amenities from these companies & these companies fund the election of their favorite U.S. congress candidate who will in return increase the defense budget & contracts will be given to these companies who funded his/her election.

- The actual motif of these companies was not to win the war in Afghanistan but to evade tax.  They poll the money from the US & Europe & invest that into Afghanistan to continue the endless war there. On August 10, 1993, President Bill Clinton signed the Omnibus Budget Reconciliation Act of 1993, one of the largest fiscal deficit-reduction packages in US fiscal history. This law raised the top individual income tax rate from 31% to 39.6%, which increased the average effective tax rate for high-income earners.
- In the war industry of USA - metal, pharmaceuticals, food processing industries, rubber, garments, small electronics, heavy machinery, software, transportation companies, energy (oil & gas), automobile.. all...industry full-scale production starts.
- Woodrow Wilson the 28th president of the USA said – America's Economic mobilization should be a part of the war plan.

# Prepare the congress support & mass sentiment in the support of the war

- ✓ Controversies that US Federal agents were involved in the planning of the Twin tower 9/11 attack. By The attack on the WTO head office, the American government will have a logic that the great American life was attacked by radical Islam. Now the very existence of Americans is in great danger.
- ✓ Despite not finding any practical evidence the CIA that Iraq was involved by any means behind the attack, how the Bush administration shifted the focus from Al-Quada from Afghanistan to Iraq –Saddam Hussein, is very mysterious & controversial.
- ✓ Right after the attack on September 28th Saudi Ambassador Prince Bandar Bin Sultan came to the white house to have a meeting with President Bush. When the President expressed his thought that Iraq must be behind this attack Bandar said, that Saudis had no evidence of any collaboration between Osama bin Laden & Iraq.
- ✓ Using false propaganda, Media reports, selling the falsehood to the world that Iraq is preparing the Weapon of mass destruction.
- ✓ The Bush administration was eager to mobilize the anguish of the 9 /11 attack to support the American invasion of Iraq.
- ✓ Christianity vs Islamism .........religious influence can bring more support.
- ✓ Both the 9/11 attack & Pearl Harbor attack were done to trigger the American people's sentiment to actively participate in the Iraq war & WW 2 respectively. Both these attack was planned to give the world a logic that, now American life is in danger, so we enter into the war actively.

# -Money and the modern Banking System-

**Karl Marx defined money as the estranged capability of humanity.**

**Money has dual nature:** Money, like light, possesses a dual nature, akin to both particles and waves. These seemingly contradictory characteristics coexist within it.

**The basics:** On one hand, money acts as a commodity, comparable to goods like wheat or corn. It can serve various purposes, from consumption to capital investment. Yet, it also functions as a medium of exchange, facilitating trade between different goods.

Historically, there has been a preference for money to be tangible, often associated with precious metals like gold, rather than intangible forms like digital or paper money. This perspective views money as a physical commodity.

**Money = transferable debt:** However, there exists an aalternative viewpoint that considers money merely as transferable debt. The liquidity of an economic system essentially embodies transferable debt, which is essentially a promise to repay a loan by a specified date.

**Crisis managment:** Before the Industrial Revolution and the establishment of modern banking systems, crises were primarily linked to natural disasters or wars. Economic forces didn't cascade into widespread collapses like dominoes. The onset of capitalism, the Industrial Revolution, and the evolution of modern banking ushered in a cycle of economic crises. This cycle led to controlled patterns of economic growth and downturns by manipulating the fiat money supply, offering a few individuals control over resource allocation.

**Debt Crisis:** Bankers effectively "time travel" into the future, extracting value from yet-to-be-created wealth to fund present production through lending. Debt crises arise when issued debts cannot be repaid. This system's peculiarity lies in the fact that those creating crises gain power and wealth, while those suffering rarely reap any benefits. Instead, they endure austerity and struggle to make ends meet.

# -Modern economics & the role of central banks-

- Central banks around the world have the crucial responsibility of fostering economic growth while simultaneously managing inflation. They accomplish this by adjusting interest rates. When interest rates are low, borrowing becomes more affordable, and saving becomes less appealing. This encourages both individuals and institutions to spend more, thereby stimulating economic activity. However, it also contributes to inflation due to the increased circulation of money.

- Conversely, when interest rates are high, borrowing becomes expensive, and saving becomes more attractive. This, in turn, motivates individuals and institutions to save rather than spend, leading to reduced economic activity. However, it also helps reduce inflation because there is less money in circulation.

- This economic model presents a significant challenge for the average person in the economy. On the other hand, it offers substantial profit opportunities for wealthy individuals and large financial institutions. In this model, where money can be readily created and injected into the system, it becomes challenging to remove excess money from circulation. From the perspective of the average person, this often results in long-term inflation.

- Until 1971, long-term inflation was not a significant issue. However, after the collapse of the gold standard in August 1971, the monetary system experienced hyperinflation and a substantial increase in asset prices.

# -The Federal Reserve- the central bank of U.S.-

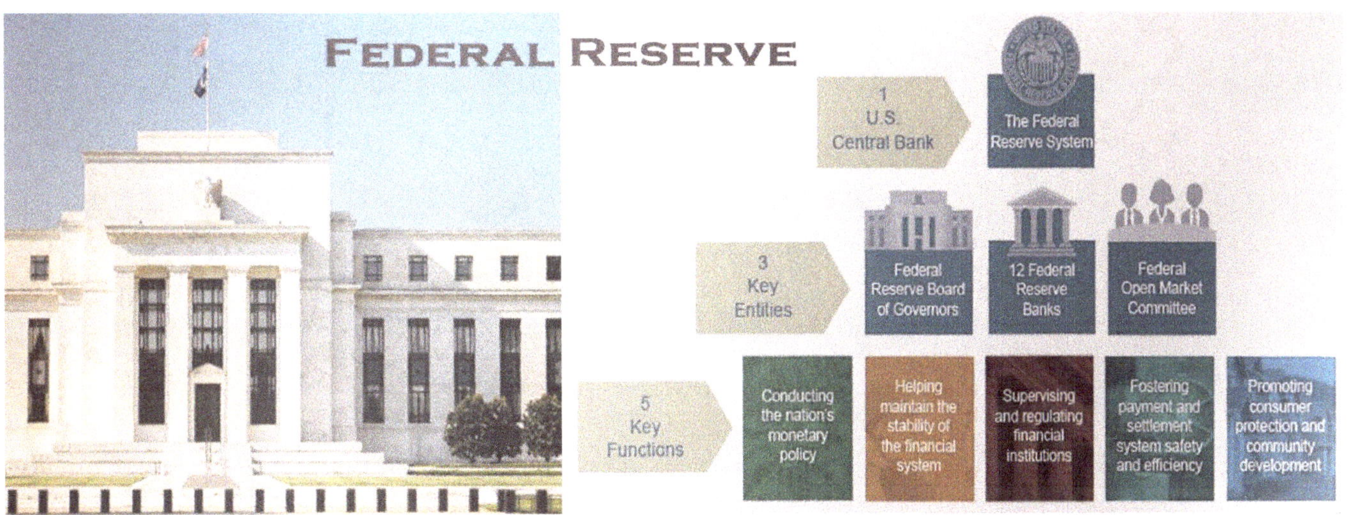

- The Federal Reserve- the central bank of the U.S. is a quasi-private quasi-government institute, but it has share holders.
- The Federal Reserve (Fed) is a network of 12 regional banks, each governed by local bankers and businessmen. These 12 regional banks collectively have a single governing body composed of seven individuals appointed by the U.S. President and confirmed by the Senate.
- To limit the President's power, they can only appoint the Fed chairman every two years for a 14-year term.
- Each regional bank is structured as a private corporation. Every nationally chartered bank is required to keep 6% of its capital in its regional reserve bank in exchange for which the private bank receives an equivalent amount of shares in that specific regional bank. These shares differ from the shares of public companies, as their price is fixed at $100 per share, and they cannot be sold or traded.
- Private banks that keep money at their regional reserve banks receive a 6% dividend per year. In one year, the U.S. Fed provided nearly $80 billion to the U.S. Treasury as profit, enabling the U.S. government to meet its expenses. Out of this, $15 billion is given to the private banks as a 6% dividend.
- The Federal Reserve was created by Congress through the Federal Reserve Act in 1913. Additionally, Congress holds the authority to pass a resolution to dissolve the Fed.
- The Fed's balance sheet comprises all the assets that the Fed has purchased with the currency notes created "out of thin air."
- The decisions of the Fed are made by the Federal Open Market Committee (FOMC), consisting of 12 members who are responsible for the monetary policy of the United States.
- In the U.S. financial system, hedge funds and asset management companies (part of the shadow banking system) play a crucial role.

# -The history of Money & U.S economic boom in last hundred years-

**U.S - GOT PHYSICAL GOLD**

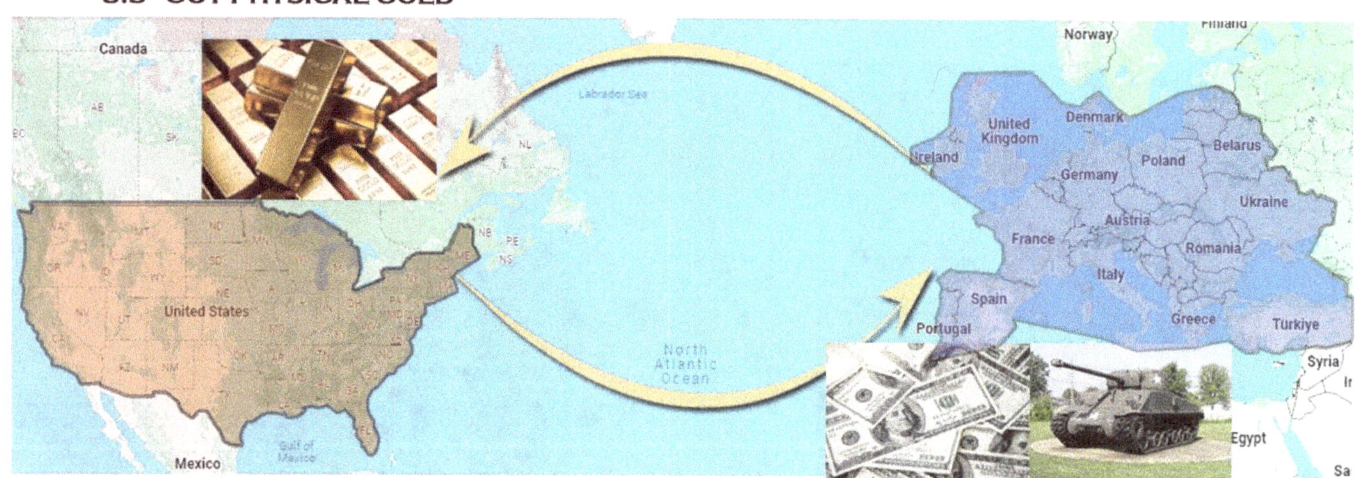


**DURING WW1 & WW2**

**EUROPE GOT ARMS & CURRENCY NOTES**

In 1913, prior to World War I, the United States initiated the "gold exchange standard," a monetary system where currency was partially backed by gold. This system was established through the US Federal Reserve Act of 1913, wherein a $50 bill was backed by an equivalent of $20 in gold, representing a 40% reserve ratio. This approach allowed the printing of a substantial amount of currency to fund the war efforts.

During both World War I and World War II, European nations paid the United States with gold to support their war endeavors. Interestingly, the United States actively participated in both wars, albeit entering at the eleventh hour in each case. This exchange of gold for funds played a crucial role in financing the wars and highlighted the global economic intricacies during those tumultuous times.

## *The Actual plan of US was-*

- By printing a substantial amount of currency and exchanging it with European countries for physical gold, these nations essentially relinquished their gold reserves to the United States and acquired large quantities of currency papers. At the conclusion of World War II, the U.S. found itself in possession of nearly two-thirds of the world's physical gold.
- During both World Wars, the U.S. war industry experienced a significant boom, with companies ranging from automobiles to arms, steel sheet manufacturers to pharmaceutical firms, all meeting the demands of the war. Capitalists, bankers, brokers, and contractors amassed enormous fortunes, contributing to a flourishing U.S. economy and robust employment rates.
- Notably, both wars were fought on European soil, sparing the American homeland.
- The U.S. entered both conflicts actively but at a later stage when other nations involved had already depleted their resources in prolonged warfare. This strategic timing made it comparatively easier for the U.S. to secure victory, delivering the final blow to an already exhausted battlefield.
- Following World War II, the Bretton Woods monetary system was established, wherein every global currency would be pegged to the U.S. dollar, and the U.S. dollar would be backed by physical gold. In practice, the nation possessing the most gold wielded significant influence over the world economy. Thus a new era of financial colonization had started.

## U.S - DURING WW1 & WW2

**GOLD STANDERD**

**WAR INDUSTRY BOOM**

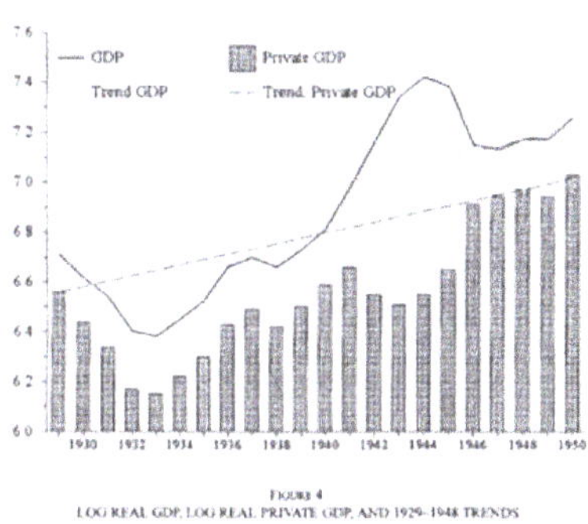


**ECONOMIC BOOM**

# -How Fiat currency is created out of thin air-

- **What is Fiat money:** _Fiat money is_ a government-issued currency that is not backed by any precious metal such as gold _or any commodity._ Practically this fiat money or fiat currency can be printed or digitally created out of thin air by the central bank of a country. For the US this task is done by Federal Reserve.
- To raise money (here we mean fiat currency paper) for her financial obligations Government issues bonds. On the behalf of US Government U.S. Department of Treasury issues Bonds (IOUs).
- **What is Bond** = Bonds are issued by governments and corporations when they want to raise money. By buying a bond, you're giving the issuer a loan, and they agree to pay you back the face value of the loan on a specific date and to pay you periodic **interest** payments along the way.
- **Government Treasury bond = Our National Debt**. The debt will be paid by you & me & our next generation by paying taxation.
- U.S. Federal Reserve writes IOUs & exchanges those IOUs with bank IOUs. Thus IOUs (banknotes printed by the Fed that banks holds become fiat currency - money) become money print fiat currency out of thin air & give loan these bonds come into the hands of banks via OMO (open market operation where these bonds are traded between treasury & banks).. at this point
- Fed & government treasury are exchanging IOUs through a middleman (bank). By repeating this process again & again Govt. treasury bonds are piled up into the Federal reserve & fiat currency or Printed bank notes or money is piled up into Govt. Treasury)
- For the public – money is a question of confidence. Any person you & I receive a banknote in the confidence that any person I meet will be willing to receive this printed banknote in exchange for commodities or services.

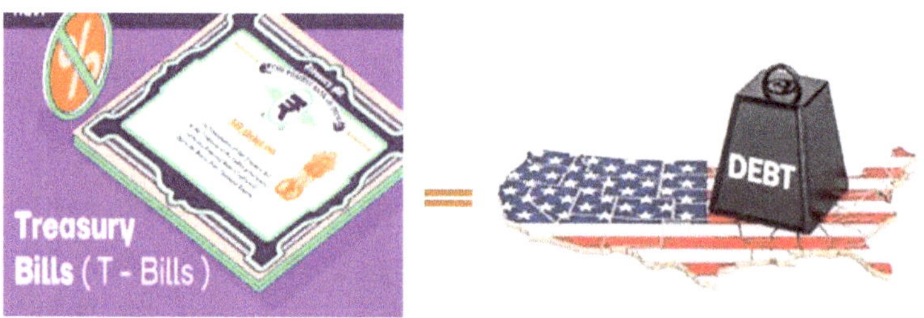

### Government Treasury bond = Our National Debt

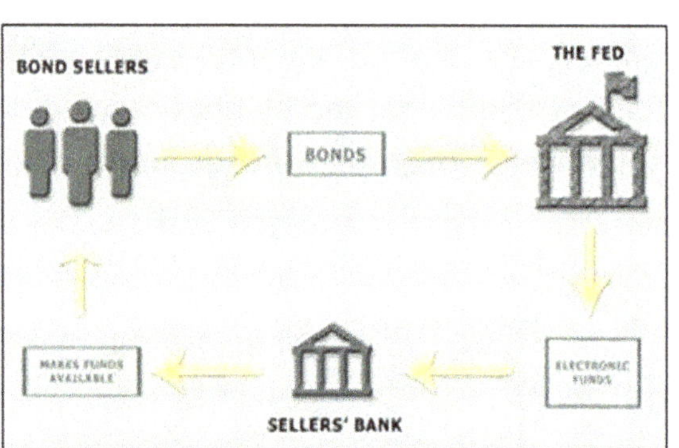



_Official Graphic From the Federal Reserve Showing How It Creates Money_



**The modern banking system is "The Creator of Money":** When banks make loans, they create money. This is because money is just an IOU. The role of the central bank is to preside over a legal order that effectively grants banks the exclusive right to create IOUs of a certain kind, ones that the government will recognize as legal tender by its willingness to accept them in payment of taxes.

There's no limit on how much banks could create, provided they can find someone willing to borrow it. They will never get caught short, for the simple reason that borrowers do not, generally speaking, take the cash and put it under their mattresses; ultimately, any money a bank loans out will just end up back in some bank again. So for the banking system as a whole, every loan just becomes another deposit.

What's more, insofar as banks do need to acquire funds from the central bank, they can borrow as much as they like; all the latter does is set the rate of interest, the cost of money, not its quantity. Since the beginning of the recession, the US and British central banks have reduced that cost to almost nothing. In fact, with **"quantitative easing"** they've been effectively pumping as much money as they can into the banks, without producing any inflationary effects.


**Why bank notes considered to be an IOU:** Banknotes are considered to be an IOU, or "I owe you," of the central bank because they represent a promise by the central bank to pay the holder of the note a certain amount of money in exchange for the note. When the central bank issues banknotes, it is essentially creating new money that enters into circulation.

The process of banknotes entering into monetary circulation typically begins with the central bank issuing new notes to commercial banks. Banknotes are considered to be an IOU of the central bank because they represent a promise by the central bank to pay the holder a certain amount of money in exchange for the note.


# -The beauty of Fractional Reserve Banking System-

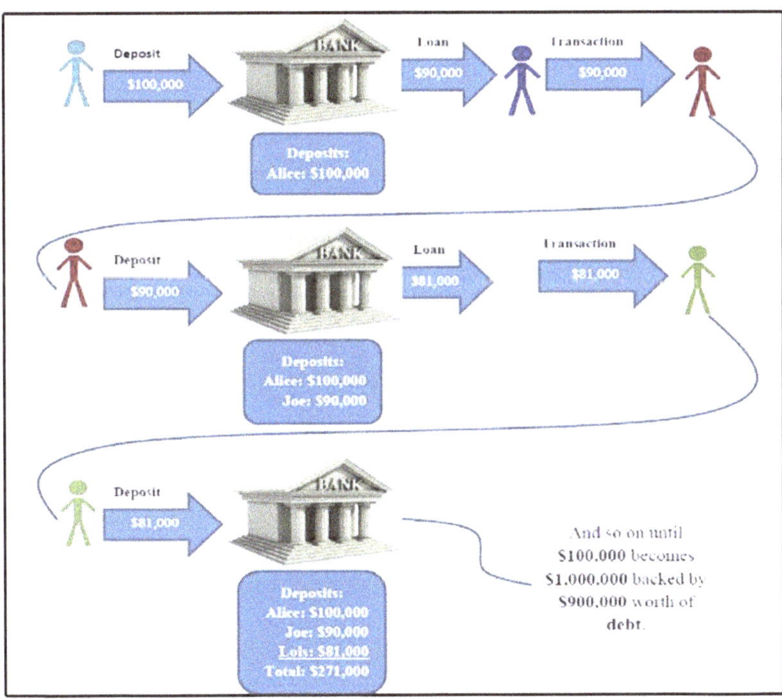


**The beauty of fractional reserve system**


**The Money multiplier:** In the United States, banks typically maintain a 10% reserve ratio. This ensures a scenario where, in cases of immediate consumer demand, banks can provide instant cash. In the modern

monetary system, banks hold the legal authority to create money, and the fractional reserve system serves as
the mechanism to essentially generate unlimited funds seemingly out of nowhere.

**Here's how it works:** When an individual deposits $100 into their bank account, the bank retains 10% of
that deposit ($10) and lends out the remaining $90 to someone else. This cycle continues as the $90 is used for
economic activities and redeposited into another bank account. Subsequently, from that $90, the bank retains
10% ($9) and lends out the rest, perpetuating this process. Thus, even though the original deposit was $100, the
cumulative effect results in a total of $271 in economic circulation (initial $100 + subsequent lending of $90 +
further lending of $81), showcasing what is known as the money multiplier effect.

<u>**The key advantages of this money multiplier system are twofold:**</u>
1. Banks have the ability to essentially create money—whether in the form of physical currency or digital
   money—seemingly out of thin air, enabling complete control over the creation and circulation of money
   within the economy.
2. This system allows for artificial management of financial crises by manipulating aspects like inflation,
   deflation, and the supply and demand of money.

# -The age of Easy money – post 2008-

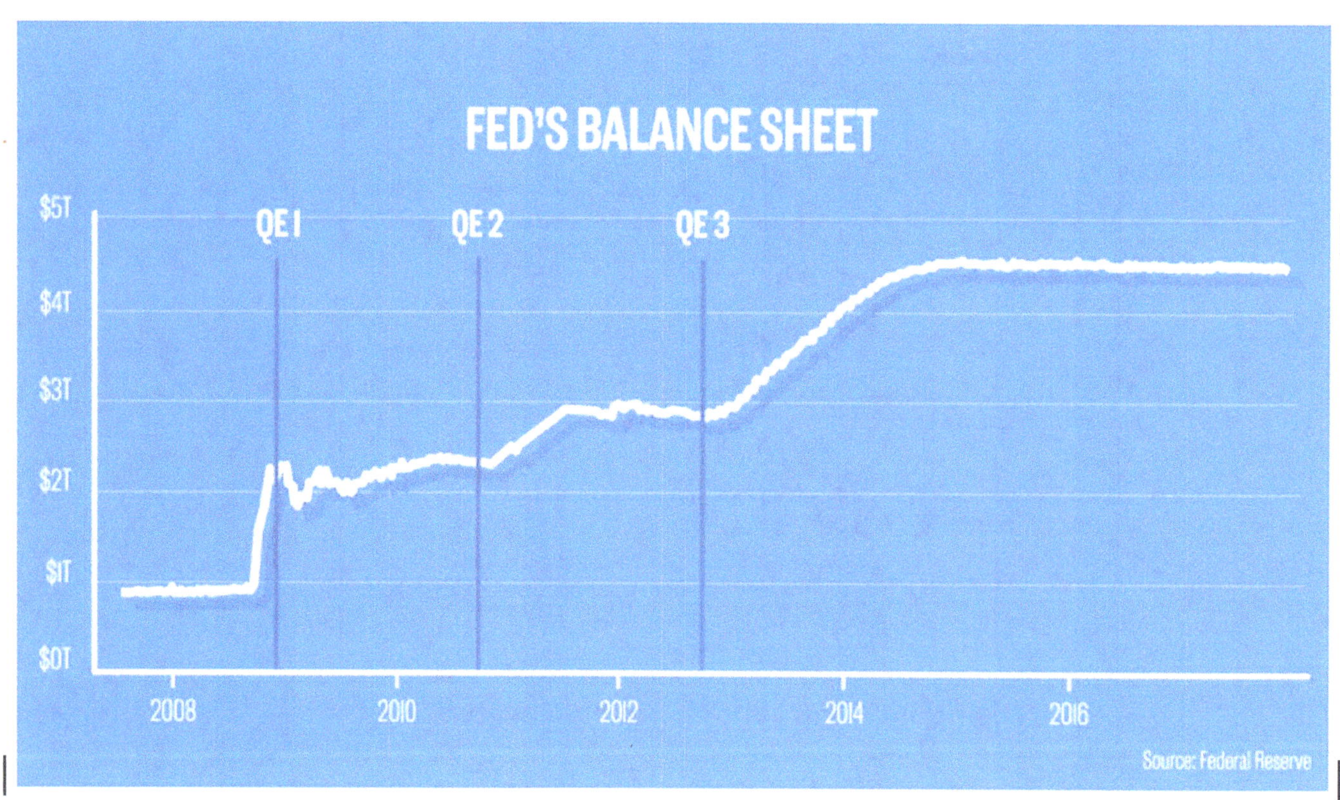

- Officilaly Fed's job is to promote employment and keep inflation in check, primarily by raising and lowering short term interest rates, making bowwrowing cheaper or more expensive.
- Fed provides the blood supply for the body of our capitalist economy.In the financial crisis of 2008, all capillaries & arteries collapsed of the financial system, to restore it Fed came out with Bail out.
- Fed has come out with Quantititive Easing **(QE),** Quantitive easing is basically injecting money into the financial system, there are two major way of QE,

  a) Lower the long term interest &

  b) Creat money by printing or electronically. Fed can create money out of thin air.
- These funds enters the economy through Open Market Operation (OMO), central bank purchases securities and assets, bonds, by it's money created from other banks. By this central bank is expanding it's balance sheet by holding financial assets- it's main objective is to lower the cost of borrowing.
- More borrowing more spending, more demand rolling the economy.
- Fed has been using all it's tool to stimulate economic activities and improve the financial market functioning.
- **QT (**quantitive tightening) is exactly the opposite of QE, contracting the money supply.

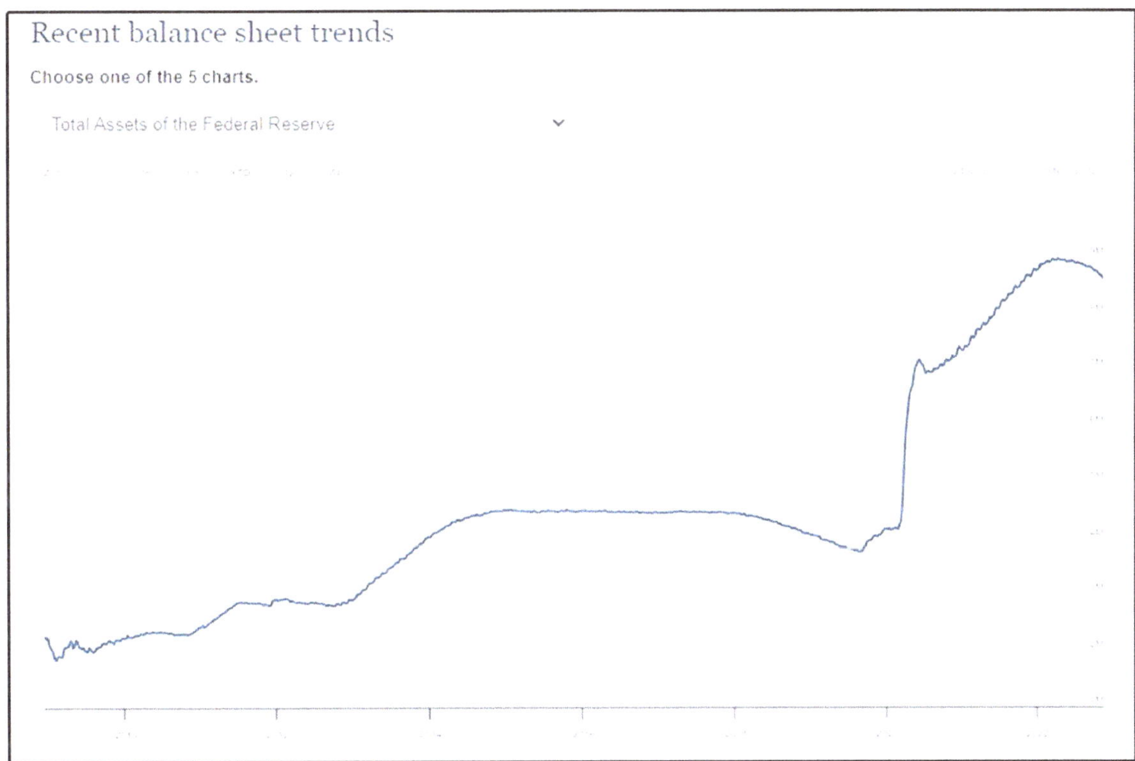


source: https://www.federalreserve.gov/

# -Shadow banking system-

**Definition of Shadow banks:** The shadow banking system is the broad collection of financial institutions and financial markets that offer the same type of services as commercial banks but that are not within the regulatory environment that traditional banks are subject to. In simple words, these are the financial institutes that act like banks are not supervised like banks.

- o Elements of the shadow banking system include mortgage lending companies, repurchase agreements, asset-backed commercial paper, hedge funds, credit insurance providers, structured investment vehicles, and money market funds.
- ✓ **Example-** asset management companies, hedge funds, private equity funds, mortgage lenders, large investment banks.
- ✓ These institutions wield significant influence over resource control and crisis management globally. However, they also serve as instruments for the financial subjugation of the masses. Their characteristics involve managing volatility and crises. They actively participate in conflicts, international border security concerns, stock market crashes, and government regime changes. This involvement creates instability and volatility in markets, thereby capitalizing on profitable investments. In post-war scenarios, following a nation's infrastructure destruction, they invest billions in infrastructure development projects and humanitarian aid programs. In essence, prolonged conflicts lead to greater devastation, which in turn presents more investment opportunities
- ✓ They engage in investments in private equities. Private equity (PE) denotes capital injections into non-publicly traded companies. Most PE firms cater to accredited investors or high-net-worth individuals. Subsequently, when these companies become established and list on the stock market, selling those shares yields profits ranging from 20 to 50 times the initial investment.
- ✓ This shadow banking system holds sway over members of the US Congress and Senate, thereby exerting considerable control over US government policymaking and decision-making processes.
- ✓ Furthermore, they wield influence over US general elections, public agendas, social media campaigns, and propagate misinformation through various media channels. Their role is pivotal in shaping public opinion.

# <u>-The next 40 years economic cycle has began-</u>

**U.S 10 year Treasury bond yeild**

Then since 1980s to 2020 next 40 years we witnessed moving down interest rate with down ward inflation. In 2020 interest rate was in "0" so this is the point from where new forty years cycle starts in where rising interest rate with rising inflation will happen.

Over the past four decades, interest rates have exhibited a consistent downward trend. The 10-year U.S. Treasury rate has served as a global benchmark for interest rates during this period.

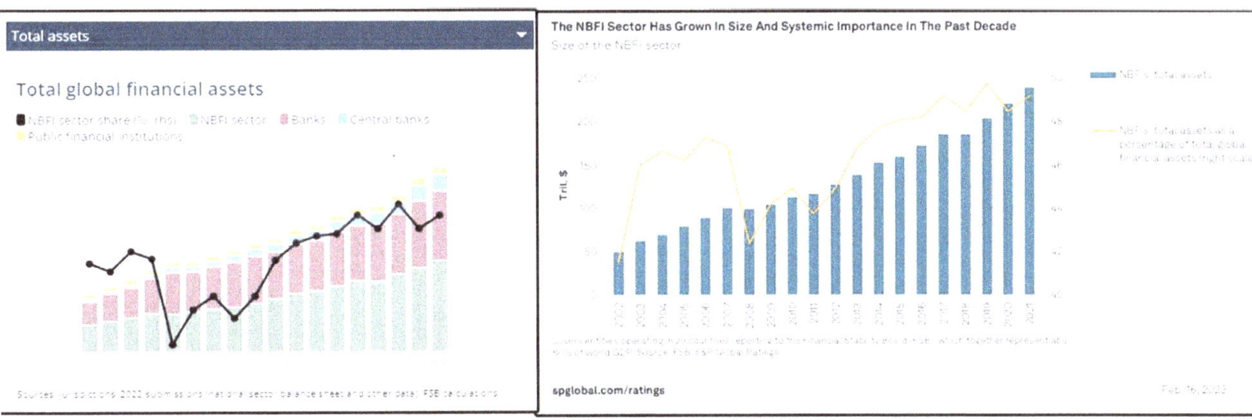



**Influence of Shadow Banking System**

Amid the 2020 pandemic, interest rates hovered near zero, effectively providing access to virtually free money. This prolonged and gradual decline in interest rates has had a profoundly stimulating effect on the economy. The availability of cheap borrowing has enabled the economy to accumulate more debt. This has implications for GDP calculations and tax revenues, alongside the upward trajectory of asset valuations.

In this extended scenario of declining interest rates, investing in assets, participating in the stock market, initiating new businesses or manufacturing units, and purchasing bonds are all favored strategies. As interest rates continue to drop over the long term, bond prices rise due to their inverse relationship with interest rates.

When observing the data, it becomes apparent that interest rates tend to operate in cycles spanning roughly 40 years, transitioning from lows to highs and then back to lows. This cyclical nature shapes financial landscapes and investor behaviors, reflecting the impact of interest rate fluctuations on various economic sectors.

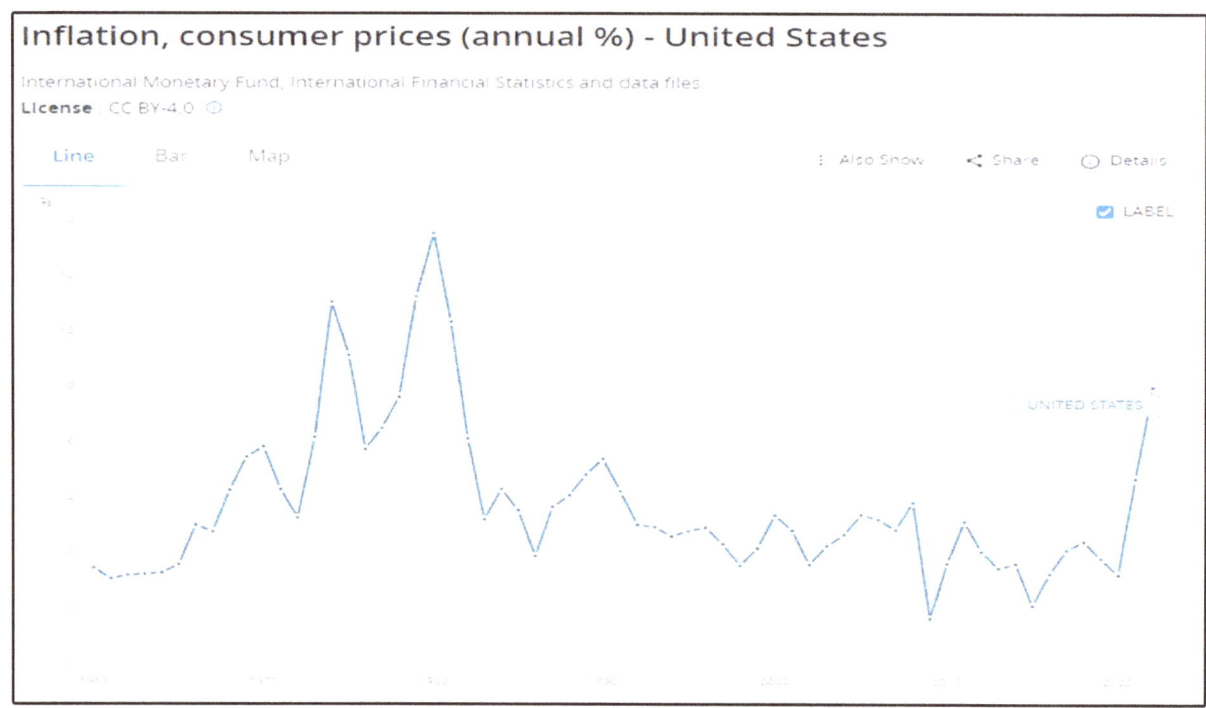


**U.S CPI Inflation from 1960 to 2023**

source:https://data.worldbank.org/

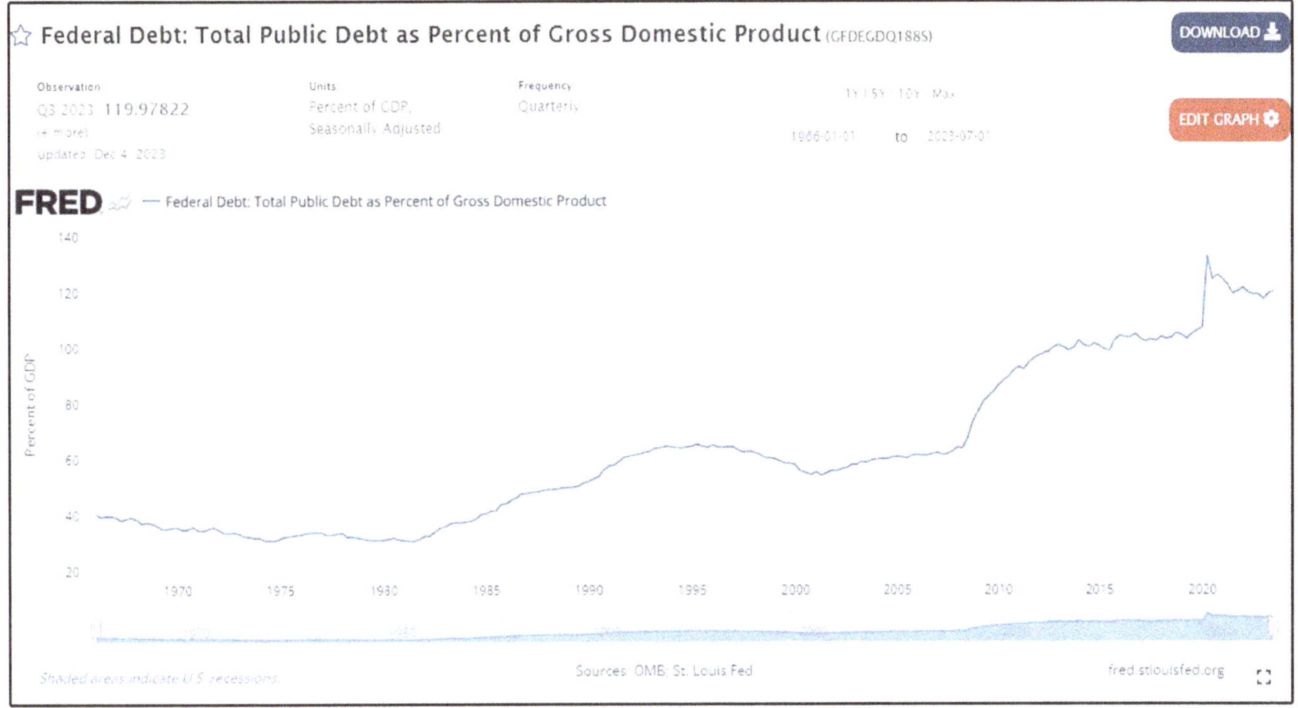


**U.S Federal Debt as % of GDP**

source:https://fred.stlouisfed.org/

# -In U.S debt to GDP ratio is too high-

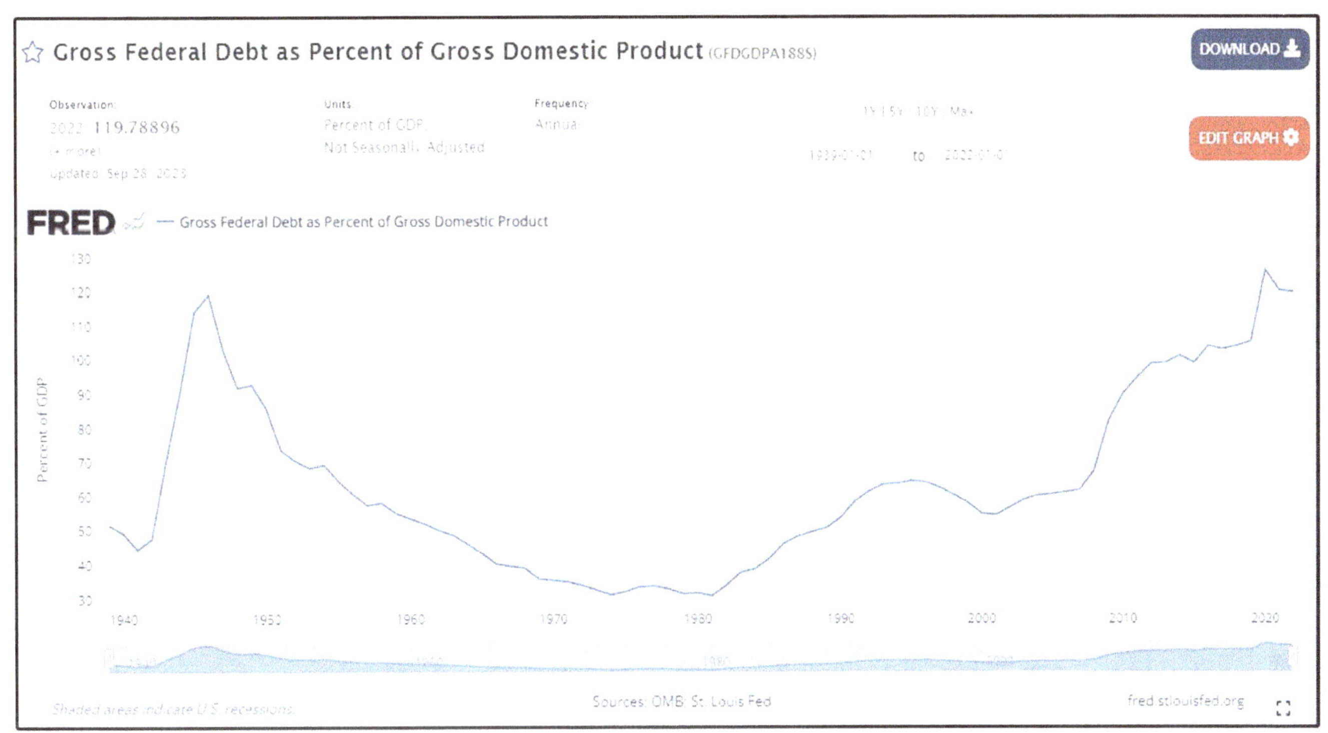


source:https://fred.stlouisfed.org/    **Gross Federal Debt as % of GDP**

- U.S has $ 32.7 Trillion debt right highest in the history now in form of U.S treasury securities.
- The current Debt to GDP ratio of us is 122.8% .
- If you borrow $ and print dollar just like US does, then what is the problem? You just print and pay the debt back. It has too problem a) you have to raise the debt ceiling b) when the printed money enters into the system this will leads to hyperinflation an affect the international exchange rate.
- A BOP deficit means a country imports more product, services and capital goods then it exports. BOP deficit occurs when (Current account receipts + capital account receipts < current account payments + capital account payments. In such BOP deficit condition in run, the country become a net consumer global economic output rather than a creator.
- Current account deficit = where the value of a county's imported goods & services > it's exports.
- One of the major reason behind the economic crisis that U.S. facing is BOP deficit for a prolonged time period.

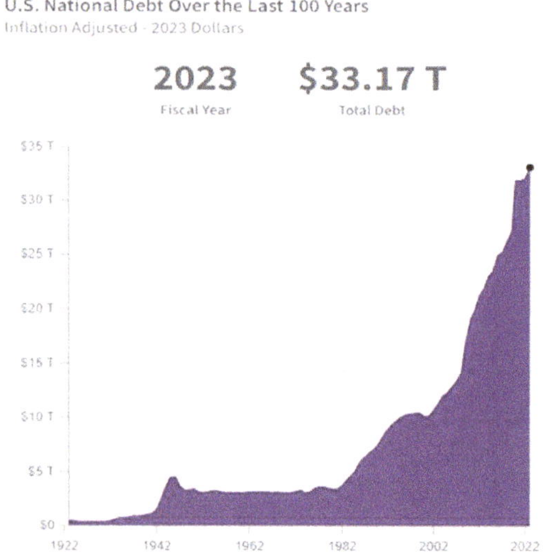


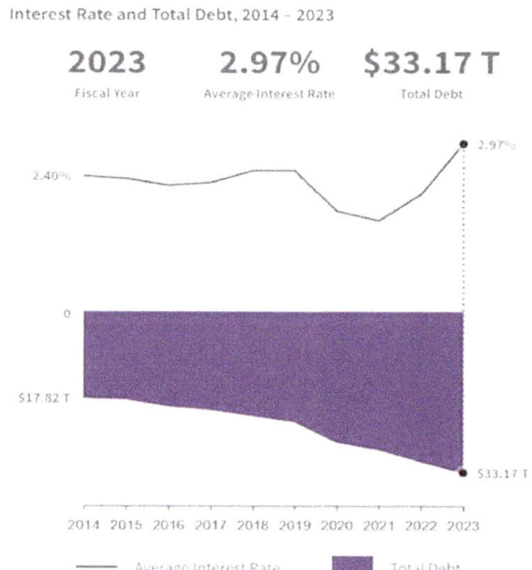

source:https://fiscaldata.treasury.gov/

# -US Debt ceiling crisis-

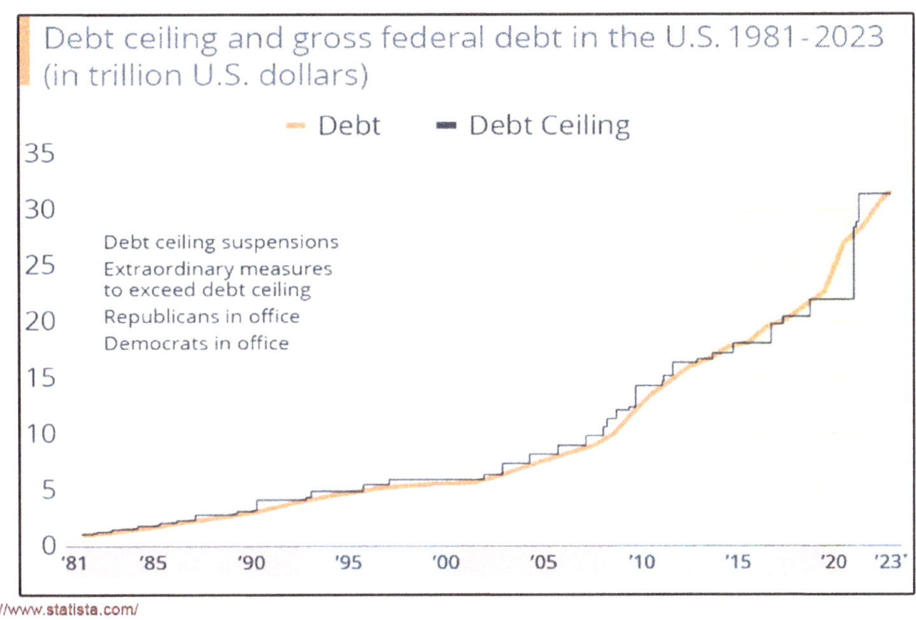



source:https://www.statista.com/

The interest expense on U.S debt alone cost the government around $ 476 billion or around 2% of the national GDP. This amount will rise to 3 % of GDP in 2024 and 4 % of GDP by 2028. Intrest payment also become the largest category of Federal spending.

Our actual plan is the dip the nation as down as possible in debt. With the increase of military expenses (the ongoing military support for Ukrain & Israle) & enlargement of social services freebees schems, U.S national national debt will pill up in a gigantic size in near future.

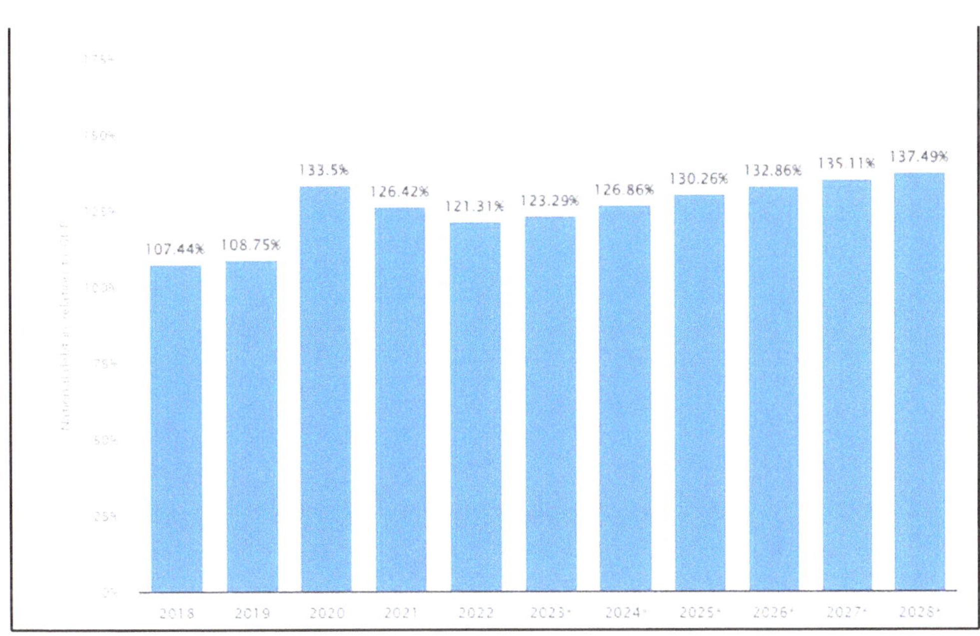



source:https://www.statista.com/

**Federal Debt as % of GDP forcast upto 2028**

source:https://www.statista.com/

**Federal Debt as % of GDP forcast upto 2028**

# -The Fiscal Dominance-

Today the Fed on one hand is trying to combat inflation by –The Federal Reserve is employing two strategies to tackle inflation: reducing their balance sheet by letting assets diminish and raising interest rates. The Fed's balance sheet holds Mortgage-Backed Securities and U.S. Treasuries, both fundamentally classified as debt. The interest paid on this $8 trillion debt serves as income for the Fed.

Simultaneously, the government's extensive deficits and exponential borrowing are fueling inflation. This excessive government spending, deficits, and borrowing outweigh the effects of Quantitative Tightening (QT) by the Fed, a phenomenon known as "Fiscal Dominance."

## Let's delve deeper into these policies:

Monetary policy, predominantly managed by central banks like the Fed, focuses on regulating the economy's money supply through tools like Quantitative Easing (QE) and Quantitative Tightening (QT). Fiscal policy, on the other hand, involves the government's financial planning, including taxation, debt issuance (like treasury bonds), social welfare spending, and other expenses.

Under Fiscal Dominance, fiscal policy wields greater influence over the economy than monetary policy. The accumulation of debt and increased deficits during Fiscal Dominance can directly lead to inflation, conflicting with the central bank's QT strategy designed to control inflation.

As the U.S. government continues to escalate deficit spending and borrowing, the nation's national debt is forecasted to reach unprecedented levels, surpassing the rate of GDP growth. The U.S. government primarily incurs three types of expenses: mandatory expenses (obligatory payments), discretionary expenses (government-driven decisions on whether to meet these expenses), and interest on previously acquired debt. Given the rising interest rates, the quantum of interest on debt is projected to surge in the near future.
Considering the trajectory of increased government borrowing, the U.S. is heading toward a Sovereign Debt crisis, entrenched in a long-term debt cycle.

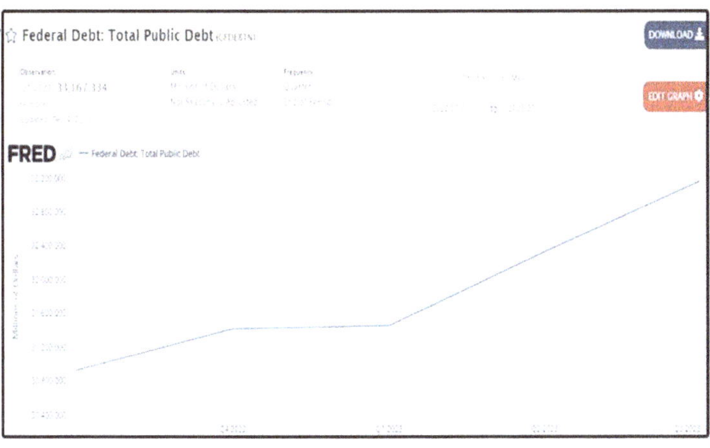

**Increasing public debt**

source:https://tradingeconomics.com/

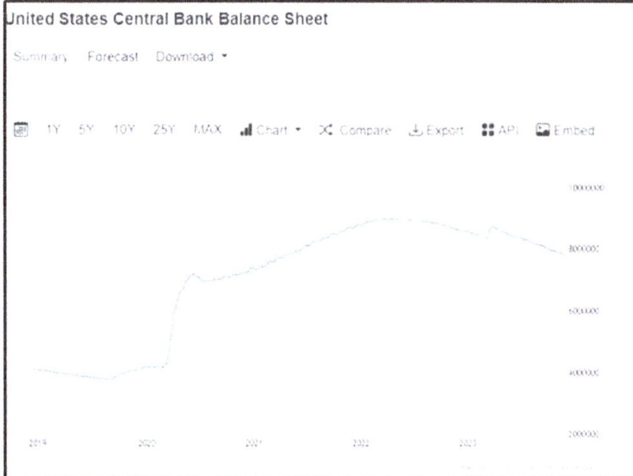

**Reducing the size of Fed balance sheet**

source:https://tradingeconomics.com/

# -Collapse of banking system, real estate, corporate debt, credit card debt-

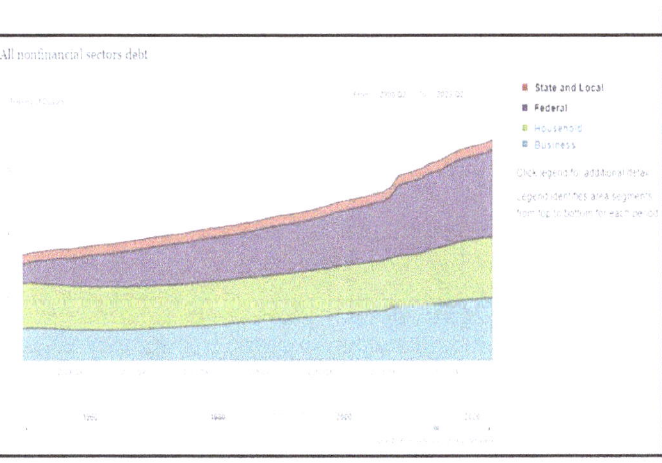

**All non-financial sector debt**

source:https://www.federalreserve.gov//

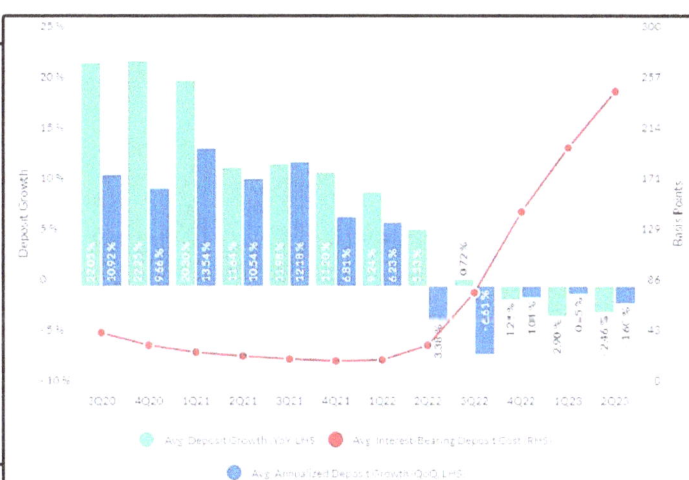

**U.S Bank deposit**

source:https://www.fitchratings.com/

**Over the next five years in the U.S**- there's a projected sequence of events: Financial reprecession leading to the potential failure of regional and mid-sized banks, subsequent consolidation within the banking sector, and an eventual transition towards adopting Digital ID and Central Bank Digital Currency (CBDC) for the tokenization of public assets.

**The new wave of Banking Crisis:** Banks operate by maintaining a fraction of customer deposits as reserves, using the remaining funds to invest in various assets, often debt instruments. The fractional reserve requirement serves to meet immediate customer withdrawal demands. However, if a significant number of customers simultaneously request withdrawals, the bank might struggle to fulfill this demand, potentially leading to a bank run scenario.

Most of the assets purchased by banks are in the form of debt instruments. With increasing interest rates, the value of these debts decreases. Banks that heavily invested in debt during periods like 2020-2021 face a challenge because the higher rates mean their asset portfolios, primarily consisting of debt, are now worth less than their initial purchase value. This has resulted in substantial unrealized losses for major banks like Bank of America.

During a scenario where numerous customers demand cash withdrawals, banks might have to sell their assets at a loss to raise the required funds, given that their asset values have declined. This situation can exacerbate the likelihood of a bank run.
The Federal Deposit Insurance Corporation (FDIC) plays a pivotal role here. It insures bank accounts up to $250,000, safeguarding deposits within this limit. However, accounts exceeding this threshold are not insured. In the event of a bank run, the solutions typically considered are either a "bailout" or a "bail-in" for the banks in distress. However, the challenge arises as around 70% of regional and medium-sized banks in America are in vulnerable positions, making it difficult for the FDIC to rescue all of them. This situation often leads to the need for bank consolidation as a possible solution.


**The Real Estate Crisis:** The current state of commercial real estate across the country is sounding alarm bells for the banking industry. This sector faces challenges like slower rent growth and increased vacancy rates. Notably, there have been defaults on loans for office spaces due to a weakened demand. Adding to this, a substantial portion of commercial mortgages, totaling $1.5 trillion, are due for refinancing within the next three years.

With these maturing loans, the anticipated new lending rates for refinancing commercial real estate loans are expected to be notably higher. According to a Morgan Stanley report, there's a potential for property prices to decline by as much as 40%. This impending crisis is especially concerning as small and regional banks are the primary source of credit for the $20 trillion commercial real estate market, holding about 80% of the sector's outstanding debt, coinciding with rising vacancy rates.


**Student Loan Crisis:** The Federal student loan debt has surpassed $1.6 trillion, impacting over 40 million Americans who are set to begin monthly payments, representing approximately 18% of the adult population. Information released by the Education Data Initiative indicates an average monthly payment of $503. This constitutes a substantial portion of an individual's income.

The burden of these repayments is expected to substantially reduce disposable income, leading to a decline in consumers' discretionary spending. Consequently, this reduction in economic activities could heighten the possibility of a recession.


**Credit Card Crisis:** The rejection rate for new loan applications has soared to its highest level, especially noticeable in the increased number of Americans being turned down when applying for new credit cards.

Lenders now demand stronger criteria such as better credit history, higher earnings, and a lower debt-to-income ratio from applicants.

Adding to this, the borrowing cost for lenders is also on the rise. These combined factors have led to a crisis scenario for the low and middle-income groups. The stringent requirements and increased borrowing costs have created significant hurdles for these segments of society, amplifying their financial challenges.

# -US and the world economy is entering in a massive recession period-

* At Davos, Swithzerland the IMF said – the world economy is heading into a worst economic headwinds since WW2.
* In WW2 or Covid the entire world basically been stuck at battlefield or at home. After the WW@ or Covid people came back to their normal life but there was no supply of commodities and goods as the global supply chain were broken.
* The demand was high enough as people return in normal life and started consuming again- this leads to hyperinflation.
* To tackle the high inflation central banks rise the interest rates, creating a massive tightening of monetary supply. Raising the cost of goods & commodities but not raising the people purchasing capacity—leads to massive recession.
* **History repeats itself:** In 1974 –Middle East oil embargo hike the oil price > rise of price of goods & commodities > inflation > rise in interest rate hike > tightening the monetary supply > leads to some massive recession.
* By rising the interest rate for the ordinary people cost of their mortgages gone up at the fastest pace. Your wages haven't kept up so, your consumption power down-you feel poorer.
* Tech companies starts laying off staff. Amazon said recently, we have hired too many people. Loss of jobs, failing of asset price.
* Every time the Fed prints money – it lowers the purchasing power of the dollar which further debasement of the currency, reflecting the devaluation of fiat currency asset price go down (real estate).
* Solution – creating digital Id, Japan, India is doing DBT (direct benefit transfer.)
* Ripple effect of laying off staff – common people losing jobs.

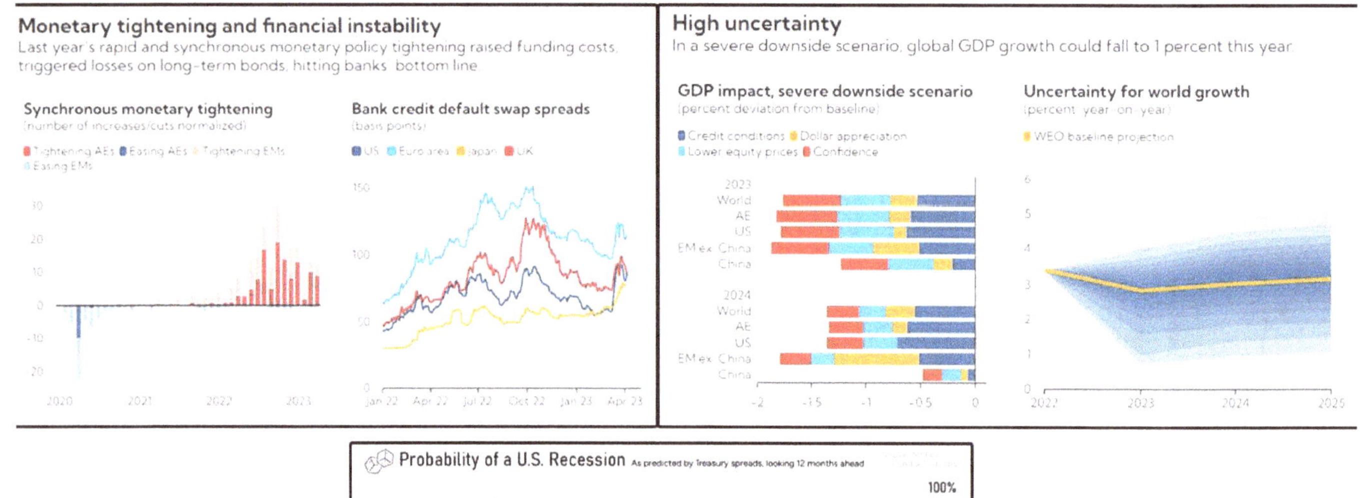


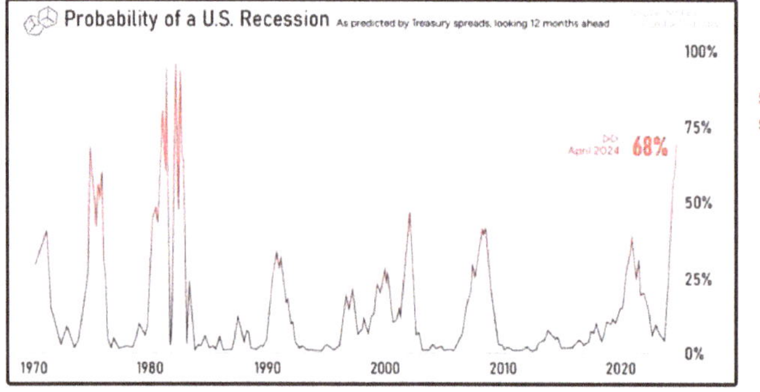


**Global Recession**
**U.S Recession**

source:https://www.fitchratings.com/
source:https://www.weforum.org/

## Are we heading towards the collapse of the "Great American Empire"?? -----Yes.

# -BANK technical terms-

**Bank Run:** A bank run occurs when customers of a bank or another financial institution simultaneously withdraw their deposits due to concerns about the institution's solvency. As more people withdraw their funds, the likelihood of default increases, leading to a cascading effect as more customers rush to withdraw their deposits.

Customers deposit their money into the bank, which then invests those funds in securities for both short-term and long-term gains. The bank typically maintains some cash to meet immediate customer demands. However, when a large number of customers try to withdraw their funds simultaneously, the bank is compelled to liquidate its investments (sell its securities) at a loss to meet the customer demand. If these losses become substantial, the bank may struggle to repay its customers, resulting in a bank run, where the bank is unable to fulfill its obligations to depositors..

**Bail Out:** A bailout refers to financial support provided to a company or country facing the threat of potential bankruptcy. This support can come in various forms, including loans, cash infusions, bonds, or stock purchases.

In the USA, the Federal Reserve and the FDIC establish relief funds to rescue a bank from bankruptcy and safeguard the savings of customers. Bailouts involve legal proceedings between the bank and the rescuing institution. In the short term, this ensures that bank customers receive their funds, and the bank avoids collapse. However, in the long term, the consequences may be felt by taxpayers and consumers through increased taxes and inflation, placing a higher burden on them.

**Bail In:** A bail-in is a mechanism to assist a financial institution on the verge of failure by requiring the cancellation of debts owed to creditors and depositors. Unlike bailouts, where external funds are used, bail-ins involve using internal funds from shareholders and depositors.

Instead of relief funds coming from outside sources, such as taxpayers, bail-ins utilize funds from within the institution, forcing bondholders and other creditors to bear some of the burden through debt write-offs or debt-to-equity conversions. In a bail-in, savers may experience losses.

According to the Dodd-Frank Wall Street Reform and Consumer Protection Act of 2010 in the US, each deposit account with less than $250,000 is protected by the FDIC. Amounts below this threshold are not subject to bail-ins. However, if an account holds more than $250,000, the entire amount or a portion of it may be used as equity, constituting a "debt-to-equity swap." In this scenario, customer funds are used to rescue the bank, and customers receive a share of the bank in return.

The Federal Reserve has been increasing interest rates to curb high inflation. This rate hike is expected to impact the bond, securities, and Treasury bill markets, potentially leading to their collapse. If banks collapse, it could trigger failures in tech companies and other small-medium businesses. The subsequent impact on the stock market could result in an economic downturn, potentially leading to a recession and, in the worst-case scenario, a short-term deprecession.

# -Europe will be entering into official recession from 2024 onwards-

The current energy crisis in Europe has been triggered by the ongoing Russia-Ukraine conflict. This conflict has disrupted the supply of crucial resources, particularly oil and gas, upon which many European nations heavily depend. As a consequence of this reliance, there's now a shortage of energy within the region. This shortage is proving to be detrimental on multiple fronts, leading to a domino effect in the economy.

One immediate and prominent effect is the surge in inflation rates across the affected countries. The scarcity of energy resources has driven up prices for essential goods and services, impacting the cost of living for citizens. Moreover, the shortage has directly impacted industries, causing a significant reduction in production and, subsequently, employment. This downturn in the industrial sector has led to job cuts and layoffs, exacerbating the already existing employment challenges.

Among the European nations, Germany, being a major industrial powerhouse, is particularly vulnerable to the repercussions of this crisis. Given its strong reliance on industrial output and its interconnectedness with the energy supply chain, the German economy is expected to face severe setbacks. The reduced industrial activity due to energy shortages will likely result in a considerable economic downturn for Germany, with potential ramifications across the broader European economic landscape.

# European nations depend on Russian energy

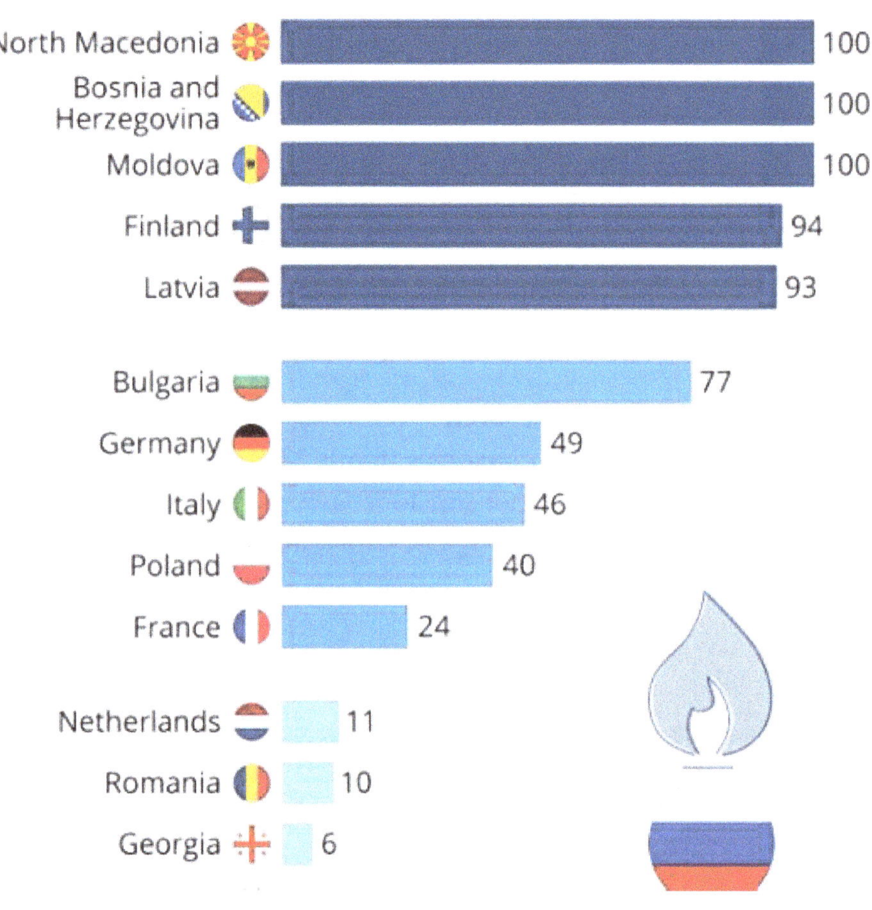


# -RISE OF THE MULTI POLAR WORLD-

**What is a multipolar world:** A multi polar world is a world where there are multiple centers of power & influence, rather than one dominant superpower or a bipolar rivalry. In a multipolar world, different regions & countries persue their own interests, values, and agendas, and they cooperte or compete with each other on varous issues.

From the 1944 onwards the world had been experiencing an unipolar power structure led by US. Where U.S at the top and all the others important contries had been following economic & political policies directed by the U.S eagrly or forcefully. Now we are in a situation where the potential superpower contries & regims are contesting each other for their survival & growth. A very dirty game has been stared where each potential country is trying to play it's card, sometimes by coordinating and some othersimes by destroying each other.

**Why they are leading towards a multiplar world:** Well, there are various reasons behind this power structure shifting. Most important of them are discussed below:

a) The west have been successful to colonise 3rd world contries for their economic & political gain. Since more than 200 years the 3$^{rd}$ world countries specially India, Africa & Middle East have been suffering enormous economic distress, poverty, malnutrition, civil wars. By these there cultural integrity & social bindings also destroyed. In spite of being a vast pool of natural resources (energy, metal, rare earth minerals) they could not grow economically-politically. Now, they releases the loos of their resources under the U.S led power structure. As the consequences of this realization they want be sovereign & self-sufficient in terms of their economic & political aspects.

b) **With the collapse of the Soviet Union (USSR), ended the bipolar system between U.S and Soviet Union and their respective allies:** For the 30 years world actors had been struggling to find the right camp for them, either U.S. or USSR. After the ending of cold war between U.S and USSR with the collapse of the USSR in 1991, a power vacuum was there for long time. This power vacuum triggers the other nations to rise as a potential super power.

c) Economic Cycle of growth & decline of U.S: 80 years. U.S economy is on the 7$^{th}$ stage. On the other hand the rise of China as a major economic and political superpower, especially after its entry into the World Trade Organisation (WTO) in 2001, and its rapid growth in the past decades. At this moment U.S and China are in economic war.

d) The emergence of the other regional powers and blocks, such as India-under Modi regim, Russia-under Putin regim, Brazil and South Africa, they have their own interest, values, agendas.

e) The challenges and opportunities of global governance, trade, security, climate change, human rights..etc.. Requires more dialogue, negotiation, and compromise among the poles of the power and another actors to resolve conflicts to achive common goals.


**Characteristics of a Multipolar world:** There are various characteristic of multipolar world, let's discuss one by one :

**Power distribution:** Unlike the unipolar world dominated by a single superpower (U.S.), the multipolar world is marked by the rise of multi influential actors. These actors can be nation-states, regional alliances. Power no longer will be concentrated in the hands of a few, but rather dispersed across various spheres of influences. Nations are figuring out economic, political & monetary policy to hold their sovereignty-cultural integrity & financial growth.

**Economic interdependence as the same time economic war:** Multiple economic powerhouses emerge, fostering trade & investments. This interdependence creates a complex web of economic relationship.

Grabbing the emerging market for finished goods & comodities is a key focus of the power full nations. This creats a economic warfare among the nations & regims to control the natural resources & potential markets.

**Security and Cooperation:** The distributed power among multiple actors creates a balance of power dynamics. Nations seeks to build alliances, partnerships based on shared economic interest & mutual security concerns. Collaboration on issues such as cross border trade, climate change, and counter terrorism has been forming.

**The potential super powers nations challenging the unipolar world:** The major nations which are challenging the unipolar power structure of the world are, India, Russia, China, South Africa, and Soudi Arabia.

**Role of India:** India is the leader of this multipolar power structure movement. Under the regim of PM Modi, India has achieved a 50 years growth trajectory in just 10 years. Energy import from Russia & soudi arabia, military cooperation with Russia, appreciation of indian currency Rupee, facilitate cross border trade in domestic currency, increase of the reserve of physical gold, con condemning the Russia in Ukranian war, rejecting the invitation to join NATO + group..And many more are the vibrant examples of India's growing power & fostering economic – political soverenity.

**Role of Russia:** Russia is the 2nd most vital actor of this multipolar power structure movement. Under the regime of Presidnt – Putin, Russia has been successful to achive a great strenth in military, economic power. Accession of Cremia in to Russian administration, war in Ukrain definatly depicts the direct confrontation of NATO in central Europe.  Sanctions by the West on Russia, force Putin to collaborate with other leaders of the world & finding other markets for its vas energy sells.

**Role of China:** China is the 3$^{rd}$ most important actor of this great reset. Being the hub of world manufacturing China is forcing digital Yuan for cross border trade & dumping U.S. treasuries on record massive scale. Accumulation of physcial gold empowers China to negotiate with its exporting markets. Growing military power on ….sea & heatwave of Tiwan-China relation also depicts the intention of China to become super power of this world.

## How they are combining together?

## Ans:  BRICS

# -BRICS-

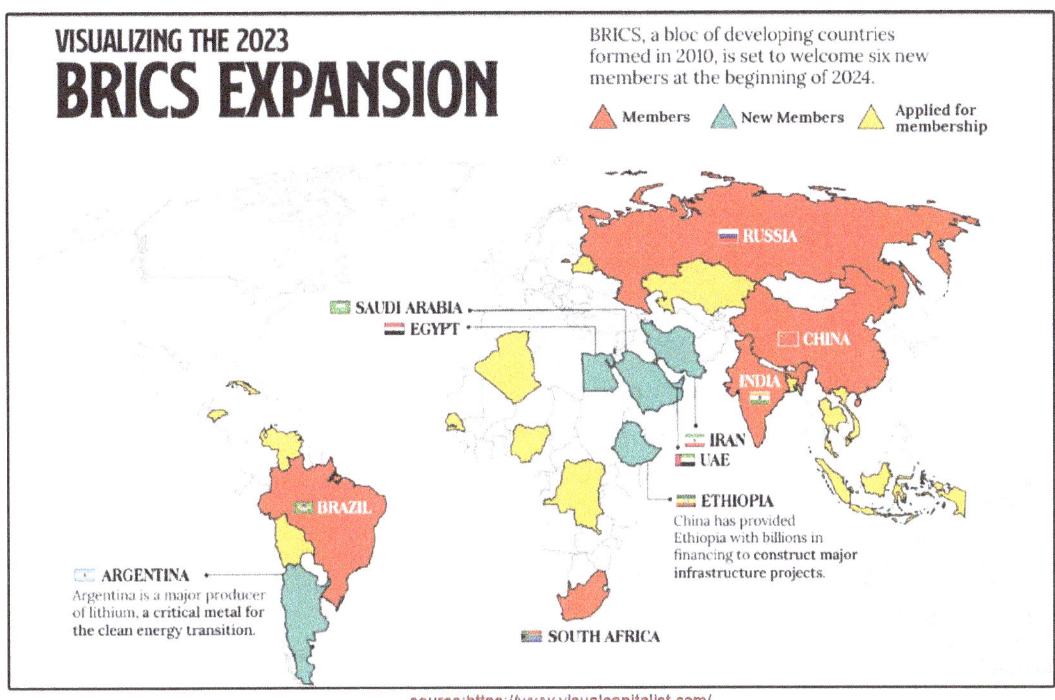



- Combined population of 3 billion people 42 % of the world population. After the joining of the six nations Argentina, Egypt, Ethiopia, Iran, Saudi Arabia and the United Arab Emirates  by the January of 2024 BRICS block will consists of near 47.3 % of the world population.
- ***Strengthening the Economic integration:*** BRICS plans to establish a powerful economic block through a free trade agreement, common currency reserve pool, and strategic partnership with other emerging economies. Their primary goal is to reduce the dependence on the US dollar $ & boost economic growth.
- They plan to establish a free trade agreement (FTA) among its member nations similar to EU (European Union) model. This would eliminate tariff and non-tariff barrires encouraging intra-brics trade.
- They plan to establish a common currency reserve pool to reduce dependence on U.S. dollar $ strengthen their bargaining power in international financial transactions.
- They are engaging in strategic partnership with other emerging economies and actively promoting South-South co-operation ties with   countries in Africa, Asia, and Latin America. The main moto behind this economic co-operation is to challenge the dominance of western power.
- ***Enhancing political co-operation:***  Brics Block aims to create a unified front on various global issues and assert their influence in international organisations such as UN, WTO, and G 20. By presenting a united voice BRICS seeks to challenge the traditional dominance of US in shaping the global politics. They are actively working on the aligning their foreign policies on "Key-International issues" such as, Climate change, Terrorism & regional conflicts. They are jointly advocating a "multi-polar world" order & greater representation of emerging economics in global decision making process though diplomatic coordination mutual support.
- BRICS is exploring the possibility of creating their own development bank named "New Development Bank". This institution would provide financial support for infrastructure development projects in BRICS

countries & other emerging countries, reducing their reliance on western power dominated financial Instititions like IMF & World Bank.

- ➢ ***Strengthening military cooperation:*** BRICS nations have recognized the importance of military power for a country's security & growth. They are enhancing military collaboration through joint exercise, technology sharing, intelligence sharing and defense procurement agreements by leaverging their combined military power. These nations are focusing on building indigenous defense equipment manufacturing hubs and reducing their reliance on foreign suppliers. Aim to enhance their self sufficiency in defense production. This would not only increase their military capability but also economic growth by creating high tech jobs & boosting domestic manufacturing industries.
- ➢ BRICS nations holds the production of the top 8 commodities globally (rice, Wheat, Corn, Soybean, Sugarcan, Palm oil, Milk, Potatoes).
- ➢ BRICS is doing pegged currency & balance will be adjusted by gold. Brics is trying to create a digital currency backed by commodities by using distributed ledger technology. That China is doing (block chain-digital Yuan). Digital currency based on block chain technology.
- ➢ ***The world is going to have a "great reset".***
- ➢ US or west countries gulo "One world Government"….tew believe kore jate all control, orders will be enjoyed by a single entity.
- ➢ But Asian super powers India, Russia, China they belive in "strategic autonomy" where they can decide their own affairs.

**BRICS Expansion:** BRIC block just admitted Argentina Iran, UAE, Saudi Arabia, Ethiopia, Egypt. These 6 countries are truly significant in their geographic reagon.

1st of all by the 2024 the BRICS block wiil be the home of nearly 46% of the world population, and it's share of global population is nearly 43%, out of top 10 oil producers in the world 6 of them are now included in BRICS. This expansion is very much focussed on natural resources specifically on energy. Vertually BRICS just created an alliance with OPEC. Let's discuss 6 new admitted countries one by one--

**Egypt:** In African continent admitting Egypt and Ethiopia is a truly strategic move. Egypt's location is very important because it allows it access to the Suez Canal.

**Ethiopia:** Ethiopia on the other hand is located in the horn of Africa. Ethiopia is one of the fastest growing economy & a large emerging market. Ethiopia also hosts the head quarter of the African Union.

**Agentina:** For Agentina, it is the 2nd largest country in South America, also extreamly rich in natural resources. Produces – Lithium- a very crucial component of green energy. Argentina is the largest producer of "Natural gas" in South America. Wheat being one of the it's main grains. Argentina playas a multidimention role by providing energy resources & food grains. As we all understand that food security is one of the biggest concerns for developing countries

**UAE and Soudi Arabia**: being the new member of BRICS – was driven by their oil producing capabilities.

: has been chosen not just for it's strategic location but also it has biggest reserve of "Natural Gas".

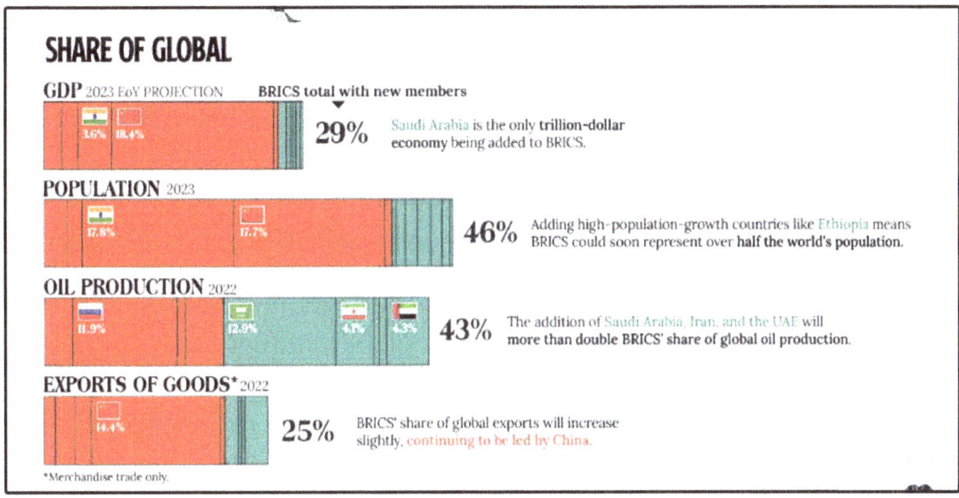


source:https://www.visualcapitalist.com/

BRICS block commette will not trade in U.S dollar $ instade in their local currencies. The global south countries are emerging them selves away from from the west now. This move will increase the demand of their local currencies thus the value of their currencies will appreciate.

Brics is a vibrant example of shifting mood geopolitically – encountering the hegemony of US led western power. They also facilitates the trade of pharmaceuticals between africa and India which was facing hindrance due to some strict international intelectual property rights by WTO. BRICS countries are formally colonised or semi colonised.

Indonesia is one of the largest reserve of Nickel, Bauxite and tin reserve. They are banning the export of raw materials. They want to export finished goods. South Africa is also planing the same. This planing requires heavy industrilsation in these countries. BRICS bank (New Development Bank) is helping these countries who are struggling to seeting up large scale industrial infrustructure & liquidity issues of their international reservs.

The BRICS expansion is a clearly signal that there is no turning back. The developing nations now have a common language they managed to find a common goal that benefits them, now they feel more united than ever.

India is leading the BRICS, The New Developmewnt bank NDB head quartered at Shanghai, will have a regional office at Gift City – Gujrat, India. It has become the financial hub for the developing nations 70% of trade and commerce and lending facilities. BRICS nations needs a player that can be trusted. As per the current senario is concern, the level of economic potential & political stability India has been achieving under Modi government—there is no doubt that India under Modi is the top most priority & trustworthy player in this room.

As we know the IMF and World Bank requires certain conditions. In contrast NDB does not not set any political or economical condition while granting any loan.  This strategy clearly breaking down the hegemony of western power backed international financial institutions. When a nation fail to repay the loan given by IMF, IMF  increases the collateral like give us your baking system, water management system, energy infrustructure or hike the interest rates,

BRI- the Belt & Road Initiative by the chinese government, basically to create an aalternative to western dominated economic and trade institution.

BRICS has become a new star & the major important countries starts to revolve around it like planets. By the encircling of BRICS these countries are developing –idea of self governance, self determination, idea for being the master of their own destiny.

Now this state led new development economic model that have power to its own people to pursue soverign development and serve the interest of domestic people.

BRICS is doing an aalternative payment system – so that the importance of SWIFT in international payment settlements will significantly down.- Anti – western alliance, Anti $ alliance- moving away from $ for international trade.

BRICS – potential powerful allainc: As per the "Petro Dollar" programme the "Oil for Sequity" programme dollarisation happened. Now BRICS is promting international trade in bilateral form, countries can use their local currency, this results de-dollarisation.

European nations rejects the condition of Putin where Putin says to European countries if you want to buy oil-gas from Russia you have to pay in either ruble or gold or in bitcoin. That is why European nations are facing major energy crisis which further results to more inflation.

There is 200% guarantee that BRICS is working for its common currency (pegged) currency which will be in picture in mid 2024. IN mid of 2024 – June July India will be busy in choosing its 20th Prime minister. Modi is very much aware of it that before his term renewal (which is 70% already predicted) he will not come in any direct challenges against western hegemony. Before his new term, replacing the U.S dollar with BRICS currency will be a direct encounter of the current international financial system. So, 90% probability is that If BRICS has to materialise its pegged currency planing in practical level that will only be executed after Modi enters into parliament in post august 2024.

As the recession in Equrope has began and U.S is facing a vertual recession which will be very prominent by the end on 2023- the status of $ will start the fall from November onwards.  From then then onwards a kick start will happen a new rally for precious metal (gold & silver).

**The Bretton Woods 3.0:**  We are witnessing a new monetary system from "East Centerd" around gold & commodities- it's like we are entering into the phase of Breet woods 3.0 where 1.0 version was in 1944 just after the end of the world war 2 (WW 2), 2.0 Brettn woods system happened in 1971 where President Nixon taken the dollar off from the gold standerd- and now version 3.0 where western super power have to come up with some solution to maintain their domination on the world economy. This Bretton Woods 3.0 can be the imposing of Digital ID and CBDC to the world's developing & potential countries by their central bank. But first & foremost we need some other tool to dismantle this global south rising, breaking these potential super power countries is a must do. Then Bretton Woods 3.0 will be smooth and each process. – And that only tool is – (world war 3) WW 3.. The solution is – engage the potential super power nations in full-scale active war so we can destroy the economy & grab their assets & resources after the end of WW 3.  The process had started after the great financial crisis of Lehman Brothers in 2008. By the Russian influence or any advisory –China is selling their gold holdings in U.S.A, thus U.S could be bring down. From hat point a new international monetary system had begun rising.

The primary plan of China & India is promote bilateral trade though NDB so U.S dollar can be by passed in international cross border trade. At present out of total trade done by BRICS Block 22 % is done by U.S dollar. But from 2024 mid onwards Bricks currency (a pegged currency backed by commodities and balanced settlements though gold) will be in active mode so, 47 % of the total trade of Bricks block will be done by their own currency

China holds a very strong position in the world economy. Since last 30 years China has become the production-manufacturing hub of the world. The whole world is very much dependent on the Chinese products – commodities. Chinese government understand this situation very well, so after the great financial crisis of Lehman Brothers China is taking big advantage of this dependence of the world consumes on Chinese goods it is strengthening its currency.

This strengthening of Chinese currency directly help China to increase it's military capacity & economic situation which ultimately leads to China's position as a global super power nation.

China & India are planning to control the natural resources of the developing nations by granting loan through Brics Bank.

China has not given military support, tanks to Russia for fighting in Ukrain war but they are financially helping Russia.

**Economic Outcome of BRICS:** The economic outcome of BRICS expansion facilitates the great reset in in world monetary architechture. Let's we understand…

A) **Anti western alliance means anti dollar alliance :** They are creating a new common currency, give it reserve status which will be backed by commodities, an alternative financial order, aalternative global payment system. They are coming together with common interest to explore opportunities for improving the stability-reliability and firmness of the global financial architechture. BRICS leaders have tasked their finance ministries, central banks to consider a local currency payment instrument and platform. This common currency is a serious cometition of U.S dollar. Through BRICS common currency & NDB the bifurcation of global monetary system is going on.

Before BRICS expansion they are holding 20% of the global out put but from january 2024 onwards with joining other oil producing countries BRICS block will be holding 42 % of the global oil output…………eta graph e dekhau.

B) **BRICS Bank is the emerging replacement of IMF:** In near future BRICS Bank (NDB) is replacing the IMF. The NDB is looking for expanding the banks membership, there are 15 countries that have formally applied for membership. NDB is capable of lending in local currencies which will help lower the cost. NDB is targeting to become the lender of choice for the developing nations & emerging markets. This will not only countering the U.S $ hegemony of world reserve currency but also reload the entier financial system.

The credit conditioning system that NDB is following is far less complex & direct, like- no politica conditions, low interest rates, longer maturity period, debt forgiveness. As a result developing nations & countries having emerging markets tend to choose NDB instade of IMF, because in every aspect of credit conditining NDB is far more attactive-satisfactory-easy-healthy for their economy.

NDB is going to play a key role in driving the De-Dollarisation. According to the BRICS Bank President .. NDB plans to lending in the South African & Brazillian currencies a "multipolar financial system" and as the result that eventually it will already lend $ 33 billion for infrustructure projects amongest members, these loans wil primarily cater the infrusture projects in developing nations.

BRICS recepntly announce that they want to industrilize the gold & tomato industry by creating ther own processing power and higger value addition products. NDB is funding infrustructural opportunities that have shifted a country's ability make sovereign & domestic policies about their own economices.

BRICS can do trade in oil & natural gas with the exchange of gold in near future may be in end of the 2024.

## C) De- dollarisantion = de- globalization = de colonization ---rise of the eastern powers.

During this kinetic war between Russia & Ukrain, Putin still selling russian oil & gas to the european countries, his demand was russian oil & gas in cxchange of Rubel or gold or Bitcoin. As the Europe rejected his demand now they buy Russian oil & gas in much higher price from Putin. Which further leads to energy crisis in Europe. As a result of this high energy price de-industrilization is happening in Europe. Europen industry has very negetivly impacted by the high energy price.

This is a start of a new monetary system coming from the east centerd around Gold & Commodities. China is able to use its own currency to trade world wide. Unlike the kinetic war between Russia & Ukrain, there is a economic war going on between China & U.S. And to strong hold its position insteade of fighting with Russia, China is supporting Russia becase they understand that U.S is the common enemy of them.

Bifurcation of world monetary system is happening. The financial war already has been stared between Western alliance & the global south.

**Political outcomes of BRICS:** The political outcome of BRICS expansion is none other than world war 3rd. let's discuss in detail.

i) ***The Big reset:*** After the end of the valuable position of American $ Chinese currency & Indian currency are the two most potential candidate to become the world reserve currency. Because to become a reserve currency for world trade, that particular currency has tobe in use in multiple nations, that is today the Chinese Yuan.

ii) ***The 3rd world war:*** Behind every kinetic war there are some ecomomic reasons. The trade war between U.S & China will lead to an active military kinetic warfare. This kinetic war will drag other pacific region countries like Japan, North Korea & South Korea.



This is a purely research & planning based highly confidential document created by Shyam Sundar Saha.
Mail id: Shyamsaha7@gmail.com, mobile no & whats app +91 9239538327, Kolkata, India.

After the complete destruction of Ukrain, NATO will be engaged in active expansion against Russia. Baltic Sea region will be the next battle ground.

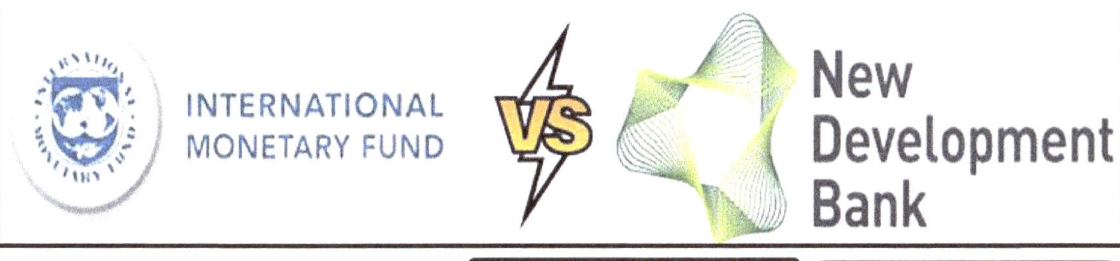


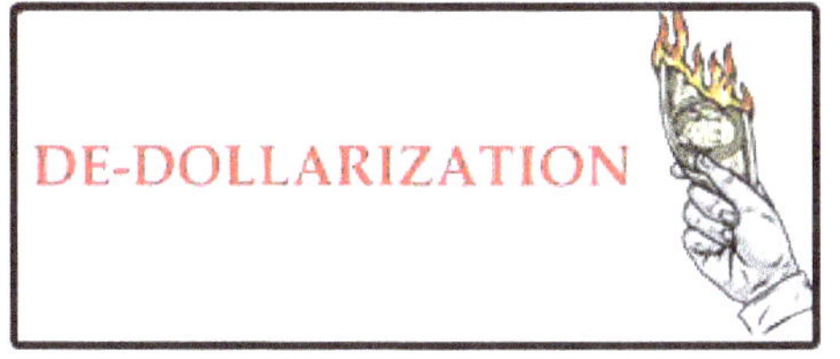

## Solution:

a) **Digital ID & CBDC.**
b) **World war 3$^{rd}$.**

# -Digital ID & CBDC-

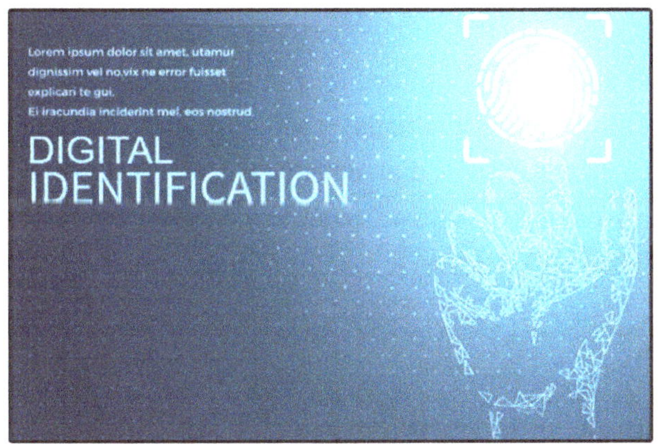

**Why it is so important to implement Digital ID & CBDC:** The Fiat currency and Fractional Reserve system represent some of the most sophisticated tools devised to subjugate people in human history. These mechanisms have facilitated the smooth financial colonization of the masses, with every country's central bank playing a pivotal role. Presently, nations across the Middle East, Africa, and Asia, historically exploited and colonized over generations, have recognized this method. Consequently, these countries are seeking aalternatives, exploring options such as replacing the IMF with the IDB, adopting gold-backed currencies, and engaging in bilateral transactions through Bitcoin exchanges. There's also an argument against granting the general public the legal right to carry or store physical gold.

One of the most significant advantages of the Fiat currency system is its capability to increase a country's national debt, enabling financial colonization. However, this isn't possible with Bitcoin or similar pegged currency systems. This realization underlines the urgency to dissuade people and nations from adopting gold-backed currency or Bitcoin. Hence, there's a pressing need for central bank digital currency (CBDC) and digital IDs for every individual.

CBDC carries another crucial advantage in the tokenization of public assets. This advancement necessitates fewer banks as smaller institutions might collapse in the looming financial reprecession. Big banks are anticipated to absorb these smaller and regional banks, leading to a series of consolidations supervised directly by central banks. Tokenization of public assets aims to track all future financial transactions efficiently.

Additionally, it's essential to differentiate between commodity credit, where individuals lend their saved money to others, and circulation credit, which involves funds generated by the commercial banking system. At present, we operate within the circulation credit system.

## -Why crypto can't be money & should not be money-

- Cryptocurrency offers the potential for a shared ledger without the need for a central authority. The collaborative process, driven by computer-based problem-solving, showcases an ingenious approach.
- It functions as an impressive system for recording contract transactions in a decentralized manner, providing equal authority over bookkeeping to all participants involved.
- Bitcoin, as a financial asset, is subject to speculation.
- In a capitalist framework, it becomes challenging to perceive crypto currency as a replacement for fiat money. Within such a system, the adjustability of the money supply is critical. Central and commercial banks are empowered by law to generate money from thin air, granting them the authority to control the expansion and contraction of the money supply.
- These actions, along with utilizing money as "debt," serve as major factors in managing financial crises. They enable the deliberate orchestration of political, economic crises, civil conflicts, changes in government regimes, funding of media and religious organizations, bank runs, kinetic wars, and the indebtedness of nations in a methodical manner. This authority allows for the creation of cycles of economic boom and recession.

## -CBDC & DIGITAL ID in detail-

- **Definition of Digital ID:** Digital ID is the way of proving that you are you. Digital ID is the digital version of your physical ID. All of us will have Digital ID issued accredited by the government and requires basic biometric information. To create biometric information this includes any physical attributes that is unique to you, such as your face, your finger print, your iris etc. Data will be stored to government computers or any private company's computer contract given by the government.
- UN should pushed its members country is to introduce Digital ID in their economies as a part of UN SDG (Sustainable Development goals) by 2030.
- WEF (World Economic Forum) is the most instrumental international organization consist of over 4000 most powerful individuals pursuing Digital ID initiative.

* By implementing Digital ID the private sector will increase in economic participation & profit making. And the public sector will increase surveillance & control over it's citizen.
* IMF is also testing for Digital ID required for governments to roll out their CBDC.
* All crypto wallet also will be connected to DI.
* UNDP is targeting launching nation DI by 2025. Report digital strategy 2022 – 2025.
* UNDP report which describes the establishment of global headquarters, country officers, regional office, policy centers, roles of public & private institutions to roll out this plan. Country officers will be the primary drivers of this program. They will be supported by the networked digital advocates with specialized training.
* At first in US Fed Now (CBDC wallet) will be launched, then Digital IDs will be created. Digital ID comes with in build Digital Wallet.
* UK is preparing to its; CBDC by 2024- Britcoin.

# -CBDC-

* **Introduction:** CBDC is a type of digital currency that is centrally controlled.
* A block chain is a type of distributed ledger technology that is decentralized, means not controlled by any one.
* A distributed database is a type of distributed ledger technology that is centralized, means it is controlled by a single individual or an institution.
* Our CBDC is actually based on a distributed data base which will be centrally controlled by the central bank.
* A person's bank accounts, fixed deposits, other assets, CBDC wallet should be linked with DI. In India this will integrate all the other IDs you have, like your health ID, voter ID, permanent account number (PAN), your addhaar number, your driving license, ration card, Thus we can monitor every single transaction happening in the economy.
* By this the government or that particular private company having the access of the data will enjoy the power to indirectly control your economic activity, purchasing power, political activity any many more. Digital ID will be a top-down approach to control one's behavlor wlth no escape.

## In India how we can force people directly or indirectly to adopt in this Digital ID & CBDC system?

*To build public support for CBDC + Digital ID, we will promote this system by presenting the following rationales:*

A. Transforming financial services through digital currency can aid individuals living in poverty and further bolster developmental initiatives, including healthcare and agriculture.

B. Central bank digital currencies are designed to enhance the current financial system by seamlessly integrating with it. CBDCs function akin to a country's national currencies and banking infrastructure.

C. Non-bank account holders can engage in transactions using CBDCs, thereby facilitating a more transparent and efficient payment system.

D. CBDCs can be exchanged for physical paper currency anytime and anywhere, ensuring flexibility in currency usage. It will help the Government to fight with black money, corruption, terrorism, drug cartels and counterfeit currency.

***Moreover:***

- The Reserve Bank of India (RBI) is contemplating launching CBDC within the "Wholesale business."
- China has already rolled out its version of a "Digital Yuan."
- In essence, CBDCs are poised to facilitate centralized control of the financial system and represent a significant step towards a predominantly cashless economy via digital payment systems.

## Promote a cashless economy by restricting the use of physical cash, the steps are as follows:

- Increase the minimum balance threshold in the bank account.
- Removing certain bank notes & metallic coins from circulation. (coin of 1, 2, 5 rupees, notes of 10,20, 50 rupees)
- Apply a withdrawal limit of cash from ATMs. (maximum 10,000 rupees in a single transaction)
- Apply a limit on the number of ATM transactions that can be performed in a month (maximum 3 transactions).
- For cheque transactions above 1 lakh rupees, you must have a Digital ID.
- In India link this Digital ID & CBDC program with the central government "Smart City" program.
- International organizations want to create a global digital system where a country's central bank will not only control the currencies but also control every asset a person owns.
- Through this system, we can restrict people's ability to acquire precious metals like gold & silver.

## Digital ID is Mandatory to avail services:

- ➢ Vote in election, Birth-death-marriage registration.
- ➢ For individual income tax return filing, GST returns millions on a monthly as well as quarterly basis for small and medium-sized businesses.
- ➢ Require compliance for hospital admissions.
- ➢ Mandate vaccinations for newborns.
- ➢ Enrollment in schools and colleges.
- ➢ Banking transactions such as NEFT, RTGS, IMPS, and UPI.
- ➢ Enable access to rations & unified health care system.
- ➢ Car insurance is mandatory for purchasing a new or pre-owned car.
- ➢ Applying for new & renewal of old driving license.
- ➢ Access to rail, air travel, and long-distance bus tickets.
- ➢ For having a broadband internet connection, mobile SIM card connection.
- ➢ Possession of certificates like ST-OBC-SC-EWS, along with labor cards.
- ➢ Offer specific benefits for individuals with disabilities, transgender individuals, the LGBT community, widows, divorced women, and those in the ST, SC, OBC, and EWS categories.
- ➢ Mandate the possession of new PAN cards, Aadhar cards, and driving licenses.
- ➢ Link access to any women empowerment schemes with compliance.

**While creating of Digital ID & CBDC wallet following documents, and information of a citizen must be included:**

**Identity information:**
➢ Birth, death, and marriage certificates.
➢ Adhaar card number, Voter ID number, PAN card number.

**General Information:** Name, address, Gender, age, parents/spouse name.

**Biometric information:** Fingerprint of all 10 fingers, any special body mark, Iris Scan, Photo.

**Financial information:**
➢ PAN,
➢ Driving License.
➢ National health ID if any.
➢ Caste Certificates.
➢ Cooking gas passbook, electricity board information & consumer number.
➢ Bank accounts, Post office accounts details,

**How 1.5 billion people in India will be integrated into this DIGITAL ID & CBDC System:**
- In India, the creation of Digital ID & CBDC wallet both will be done in a single shot in one attempt under the office of "BHARAT SAHAYK KENDRA" – Apni ajazi apne hat, apni unnati desh ke sath. Social credit score & carbon credit score will be linked to this Digital ID when creating of this account.
- The government will pool a vast amount of data information on every single citizen. This requires a huge & high-capacity data center which will be created through Block Chain Technology. This data center will be directly linked to the Central Bank RBI. Thus the central bank & government will have access to each & every behavior of its citizens.
- This data center will be owned by a fully private foreign entity or company. And we need some changes in the central banking system & parliamentary system of India to have full control over India. This has been discussed in a separate part of this document.
- Explain the 73rd and 74th amendments of Indian constitutions. Which are the blood circulation system including capillaries (smallest blood vessels in the human body) a.

¬ There will be two kinds of office. One is **"permanent sahayak Kendra"** and therother one is **"mobile shayak Kendra".**

¬ **permanent sahayak Kendra :**
1. **In Urban areas:** Each municipality, one school under each municipality, One SBI branch in each municipality, each Head post office, Each railway junction, and each SDO office, will have a permanent "Bharat Sahayak Kendra".
2. In rural areas: each BDO office.

¬ **Mobile Sahayak Kendra :**
1. In Urban areas, 3-day mobile camps will be organized at the ward level under a particular municipality.
2. In Rural areas, 3-day mobile camps will be organized at the Gram panchayat level under a particular Block (Tehsil).

# -Social credit score-

The implementation of a social credit scoring system for citizens will evaluate their compliance with civil duties. The fundamental idea is to observe and guide citizens' behavior.

The parameters for the social credit score are categorized into individual and collective responsibilities:

## Individual Responsibility:

- Citizens are required to vote and participate in government-provided social service schemes.
- Adherence to traffic rules is mandatory.
- Expressing seditious statements against the government is prohibited.
- Ownership of excessive physical gold and real estate is restricted.
- Encouragement for blood and organ donation.
- Mandatory provision of free service to the government for a specified period.

## Collective Responsibility:

- Restriction on gatherings or travel in specific areas after 10 PM.
- Prohibition against public agitation against the government.
- Restrictions on trolling, mocking, or criticizing the government on social media or other platforms.

The approach follows a 'carrot and stick' formula: positive behavior will be rewarded, while negative behavior will be penalized. Good behavior, such as blood donation or volunteering for the government, will result in a higher social credit score.

Positive actions will be rewarded with benefits like reduced electricity bills, access to higher education, easier access to public facilities, free gym memberships, and preferential treatment for loans and travel bookings.

Conversely, negative actions will result in punishments such as limited access to public amenities, social services, higher taxes or fines, and reduced chances of loan approvals.

The rationale behind implementing the social credit scoring system is its benefits for citizens and the economy, including reduced crime rates, enhanced security, economic growth, financial stability, consumer protection, promotion of civic behavior and responsibility, improved administrative efficiency, reduced corruption, and better political engagement.

# -China is the leader of rolling out CBDC-

- The name of China's CBDC is "Digital Youn". Digital ID + CBDC is a surveillance monitoring system, controlling the behavior of citizens.
- This is an instantaneous round-the-clock payment system at a much lower cost and greater access to financial services for retail & whole participants.
- BY implementing this, DBT (Direct Benefit Transfer) from the government to citizens is much easier.
- CBDC gives a balance between controllable anonymity and anti-money laundering.
- Counter-terrorist financing, online gambling, Easy tax payments, tracking electronic criminal activities will be much easier.
- This would allow the central banks to create a massive data center with real-time visibility into its citizen's economic activities. For this a vast amount of data will be collected from the users of every single transaction and a customer's personal details.With the help of this system, the government can freeze the assets of a criminal.
- China is also working in BSN (Blockchain-Based Service Network) – deployment of blockchain technology in the cloud computers.

# -The World War 3<sup>rd</sup>-

**The following things are the consequences when a country is involved in active war:**
- Scarcity of daily lifestyle amenities. The price rise of goods & commodities leads to high inflation.
- Due to high inflation the value of public savings is wiped out.
- To fund the war that country needs more money compared to regular financial obligation, for the central bank of that country print huge amount of currency notes out of thin air which further leads to currency devaluation.

- To fund the war country's deficit spending rises. It has to borrow from foreign institutions, and as a result, the National Debt of that country rises sharply.
- The price of essential commodities like food grains & oil skyrocketed.
- Drain of resources (land, infrastructure, energy, human capital..etc).
- Foreign exchange reserve depletes & physical gold holdings deplete that country.

# - Russia-Ukraine kinetic war -

## Russia – Ukraine conflict:

- Putin wants to rebuild Russia as the global leader. Putin starts to invade former Soviet territories- 2014- Cremia, 2022- Ukraine, Georgia-2008,
- Actually this war was started in way back 2014 when by the diplomacy of Washington democratically elected govermnet was overthrown by "Maidan Revolution or the Ukrainian Revolution, took place in Ukraine in February 2014" Removal of President Viktor Yanukovych and put puppet government in Ukrain.
- To increase the arms-amunation business NATO has to to be extended eastward. President Viktor Yanukovych was playing a nuetral game balancing both side Putin on one side NATO on the other. That is why it was so important for washinton to remove him & create tension in that region.
- Putin understood the danger of Ukrainian government regim change onto a Pro western. In last two weeks of February and first two weeks of march Putin made a significant move by Annexation of Crimea into Russia sequring the trade route in Black sea.

**NATO:** NATO, formed in 1949 after World War II due to the fear of the Soviet Union, is a collective security system where member states agree to defend each other. Membership has expanded over the years, with 31 countries currently involved. The organization acts as a deterrent against potential threats and maintains stability in Europe, based on shared democratic values.

However, NATO also faces criticisms. Some argue it's costly and no longer necessary post-Cold War. Others view it as an aggressive alliance expanding influence rather than deterring aggrecession. There are concerns about its effectiveness in preventing conflicts like those in Bosnia, Kosovo, and Ukraine.

The financial burden of NATO falls heavily on the United States, which contributes significantly more than other member states, raising questions about its necessity and the motivations behind this disproportionate spending.

Current tensions regarding NATO's expansion towards Russia's borders, specifically Ukraine's potential membership, have heightened concerns. This move could potentially trigger conflicts as per NATO's treaty stating an attack on any member is an attack on all.

The geopolitical landscape involving NATO, BRICS (Brazil, Russia, India, China, South Africa), and potential adversaries like Russia and China raises questions about power dynamics and the risk of conflict. There are comparisons made in military capabilities, but concerns linger over non-conventional threats like cyber and biowarfare.

The U.S. prioritizes its own interests and security, staying vigilant against potential adversaries and carefully considering the implications of its alliances and actions within NATO.

## The Warsaw pack:

- Warsaw Treaty Organization (also known as the Warsaw Pact) was a political and military alliance established on May 14, 1955, between the Soviet Union and several Eastern European countries. The Soviet Union formed this alliance as a counterbalance to the North Atlantic Treaty Organization (NATO),
- When the Federal Republic of Germany entered NATO in early May 1955, the Soviets feared the consequences of a strengthened NATO and a rearmed West Germany and hoped that the Warsaw Treaty Organization could both contain West Germany and negotiate with NATO as an equal partner.
- The original signatories to the Warsaw Treaty Organization were the Soviet Union, Albania, Poland, Czechoslovakia, Hungary, Bulgaria, Romania, and the German Democratic Republic. Although the members of the Warsaw Pact pledged to defend each other if one or more of them came under attack, emphasized non-interference in the internal affairs of its members, and supposedly organized itself around collective decision-making, the Soviet Union ultimately controlled most of the Pact's decisions.

The lack of political stability and inhibited economic growth in Middle Eastern countries can be attributed to their strategic geographical positioning and rich energy reserves. This same rationale extends to African and Latin American nations. Should these countries achieve economic self-sufficiency and sovereignty in their domestic and international policies, our ability to exploit them would diminish.

Eurasian nations boast vast farmlands yielding significant quantities of staple food grains, constituting a substantial market for finished goods. Ukraine, positioned at the heart of these Eurasian countries, plays a pivotal role. Therefore, fostering political stability and economic growth in Ukraine becomes imperative.

In the ongoing Russia-Ukraine conflict, prolonged kinetic warfare would devastate Ukraine on multiple fronts—financially, in terms of human resources, and infrastructure.

## Sustained conflict will yield several outcomes:

a. Ukraine's destruction across the financial, human resource, and infrastructural aspects.
b. Escalating energy prices in European and Eurasian countries leading to infrastructure and manufacturing degradation, potentially resulting in de-industrialization.
c. Economic recession is already underway in this region, marked by food and energy shortages. The impending winter season could exacerbate this situation.
d. Prolonged engagement in war with Russia would divert the government machinery's focus and drain its resources.
e. Post the destruction of Ukraine, NATO's role might escalate to fill the gap, potentially intensifying tensions, particularly in the Baltic Sea region.
f. In next 3 to 5 years Ukraine must not join NATO, so we will be able to continue this conflict just like as it is going on.

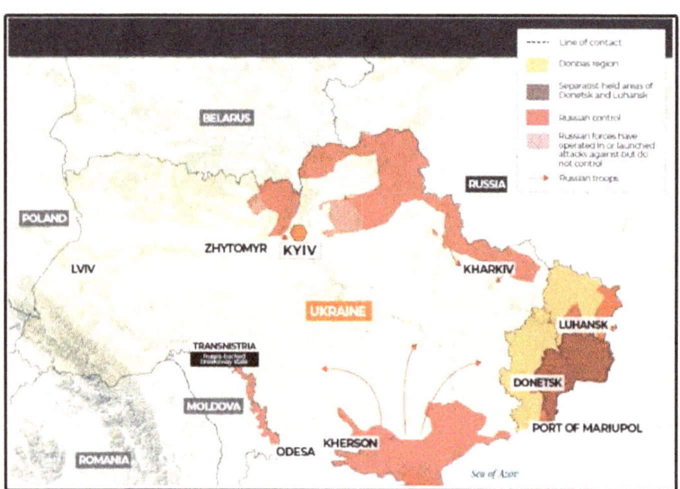

To the the current situation of international politics, today's economic warfare between the U.S., China, Russia, African global south will lead to kinetic military warfare. In the future, if the deep states want to maintain its controlling position world war 3 is the only way out.

# -The Israel-Palestine conflict-

The Israel-Palestine conflict embodies an age-old divergence and discontent in the Middle East, primarily among Jewish, Muslim, Shia, and Sunni populations. What's intriguing is how a religious issue or sentiment has morphed into an enduring identity crisis, sparking a struggle for survival. From this conflict, economic and political benefits have been extracted—a stark demonstration of this transformation.

The Middle East, given its strategic location and abundant energy resources, notably the Suez Canal serving as a pivotal point for global cargo transportation, has played a significant role in the world's economy and politics for over two centuries. The creation of a Jewish state in the midst of a predominantly Muslim area, orchestrated by the CIA, stands out as a strategic maneuver. Moreover, the CIA's involvement in fostering MOSSAD, among the world's most proficient intelligence agencies, from Israel, further underscores this strategic play.

The ongoing perpetual identity crisis and survival struggle between Israel and Palestine have presented substantial profit opportunities for banks and manufacturers of military equipment. Sadly, this conflict, while deeply rooted in historical and religious contexts, has also become a profitable business model, undermining genuine efforts toward resolution.

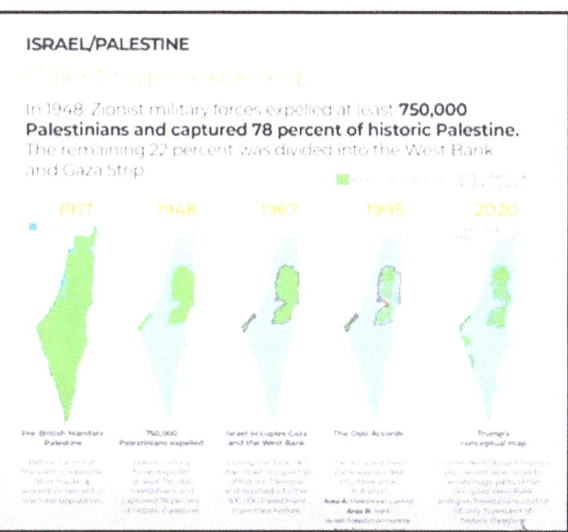


# -CHINA - TAIWAN WAR-

**Why Taiwan & Taiwan Strait is so important for China?** For China, the importance of Taiwan goes beyond the usual rhetoric of nationalism, it is strategic.
Geopolitically, Taiwan occupies a pivotal position at the heart of the initial chain of islands in the western Pacific. It is officially known as the Republic of China (ROC) and is geographically separated from mainland China by the Taiwan Strait. Throughout history, Taiwan's strategic significance, situated off the coast of China and between Northeast and Southeast Asia, has served as a multifaceted advantage for regional powers in both offensive and defensive contexts.

**The Strategic importance of Taiwan due to its geographic location**: Geopolitically, Taiwan lies at the center of the first chain of islands in the western Pacific. Taiwan's location on the periphery of the shipping lanes in the South China Sea places it at a mere distance of 100 miles from the Chinese coast, 200 miles south of the Philippines, around 900 miles from Vietnam, just under 1,000 miles from the Spratly Islands, and approximately 700 miles from the Japanese archipelago.

**The Economic Significance of Taiwan & Taiwan Strait:** Although Taiwan may appear to be a small island, with a population of 23 million and its robust economy hold significant influence in the world economy. Presently, Taiwan stands as the 11th largest trading partner of the United States, the 22nd largest global economy, and a dominant player in the global semiconductor chip markets.
The Taiwan Strait is recognized as one of the most bustling shipping lanes in the region, facilitating the transit of nearly 90% of Chinese, Japanese, and Korean trade towards Asia, the Middle East, and India. This vital waterway serves as a lifeline for the US, Japan, South Korea, and numerous other countries, allowing them to transport their goods worldwide, and vice versa.

China, given that its major ports are situated in the Yellow Sea, places immense value on trade passing through the Taiwan Strait. On one hand, China aims to exert control over the trade routes through the strait, while on the other hand, it seeks to safeguard its shipping lanes that traverse this critical passage.

## It is so important for China to control Taiwan from multiple angles.

**One China Policy:** According to the one-China principle, Taiwan is considered an integral and inseparable part of China, and the sole legal government representing the entirety of China is the Government of the People's Republic of China. This principle is firmly established and regarded as an unshakable foundation in the context of the de facto relationship between China and Taiwan. The belief is that Taiwan has been historically linked to China since ancient times.

**Strategic & economic reason:** If China were to dominate the South China Sea, major US allies like Japan could face disruptions in trade and supplies, affecting their economic and strategic interests. Moreover, China's control over the region would grant it greater power projection not only in the Pacific but also over Japan, the Philippines, and other ASEAN countries.

By gaining control of Taiwan, China could enhance its operations in the South China Sea and more assertively advance its territorial and maritime claims against countries like the Philippines, Vietnam, Malaysia, and Brunei. This would bolster China's "nine-dash line" claim, making it more enforceable and intensifying regional tensions.

From a naval and military standpoint, Taiwan's control would bestow China with a substantial strategic asset and pose a threat to the entire Southeast and Northeast Asian regions, as well as to the interests of the United States.

Based on the information presented above, it appears that China is attempting to seize Taiwan and bring it under its complete control. There is a concern that this ongoing China-Taiwan conflict could escalate into an active military confrontation shortly.

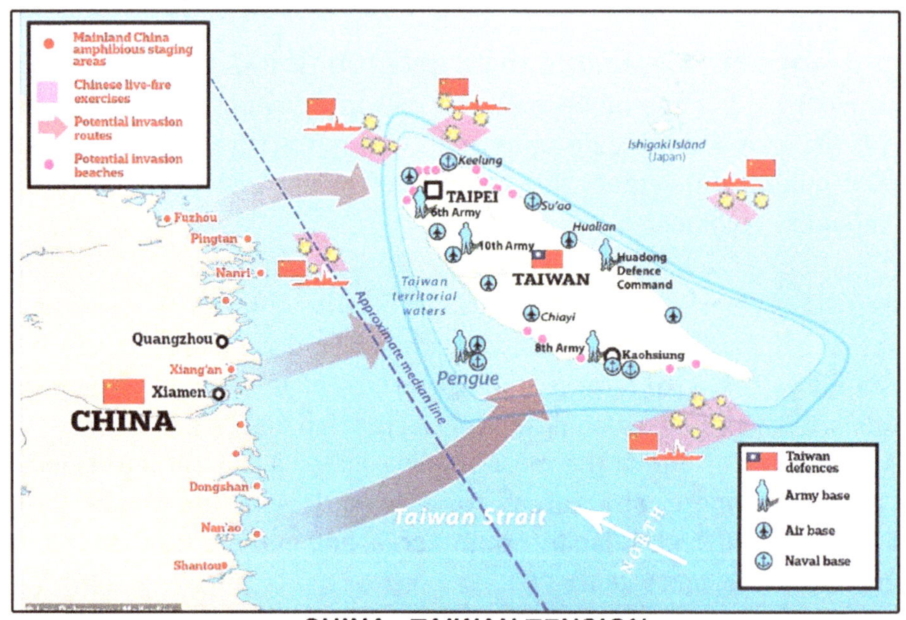


**CHINA - TAIWAN TENSION**

source:https://www.purple-trading.com/

**So why not let's start the War, a war which will be highly beneficial for us.**

- **Step 1 = Dissemination of false propaganda and the exertion of pressure on the Taiwanese government with the aim of provoking China.**
    - In the Taiwan Strait, a Chinese fishing vessel, armed with military ammunition, launched an attack on a Taiwan military boat, resulting in the tragic loss of tens of military personnel.
    - Thus, a situation will be created where Taiwan's Government feel a serious threat to its sovereignty.
    - As, US Govt has very close ties with Taiwan, US security advisors will pressurize Taiwan, this Chines attack is a serious threat to Taiwan.
- **Step 2 = US will pressurize Taiwan Government officials to counterattack an active military strike on Chinese military vessels & import shipment on Taiwan Strait.**
    - We have to make Taiwan believe that, China is now playing actively to invade on Taiwan & the existence of Taiwan is in serious danger.
    - We have to create a situation for Taiwan, where Taiwan will have only two choices, either get invaded by China or strike active attack on China.
- **Step 3 = A series of small military attacks will be done by Taiwan…over a long period of time.**
    - We want a series of small military retaliation by Taiwan to China military boats & shipments, till China bound or forced to eliminate this risk by attacking Taiwan.
    - The primary objective is to indirectly compel China to retaliate against these attacks, as China perceives them as a significant threat to its sovereignty, military expansion, and economic prosperity.
- **Step 4 = China will actively retaliate with heavy military power, making serious damage to Taiwan.**
- **Step 5 = US & its allies will form a collaboration to rescue Taiwan from the bottleneck situation.**
    - US & its allies will provide Financial support in form of loans & military support to Taiwan to fight back.
    - This military support will consist of mainly ground military forces & small vessels equipped with short range rocket launchers.
    - We want this war to be continued for long time.. at least for next 3 to 4 years.
- **Step 5 = pressurize Taiwan to shift its Semiconductor industry to somewhere else**, as the industrial belts will seriously under threat of China missile attack & air attack.



This is a purely research & planning based highly confidential document created by Shyam Sundar Saha.
Mail id: Shyamsaha7@gmail.com, mobile no & whats app +91 9239538327, Kolkata, India.

# -CHINA-MYANMER RELATION-

China and Myanmar's relations encompass trade, investments, and strategic interests. China and Myanmar share a 2129-km-long border with deep historical and cultural ties. China is Myanmar's largest trading partner, accounting for about USD 12 billion out of the total USD 36 billion bilateral trade. Myanmar imports machinery, metal products, vehicles, and telecommunication equipment from China. China imports refined tin and rare earth minerals from Myanmar, crucial for electronics and military equipment production.

China heavily invests in Myanmar's infrastructure, including a natural gas and oil pipeline connecting Kyaukphyu to China's Yunan region for USD 4.5 billion. China dominates Myanmar's electricity sector and plans a USD 2.57 billion LNG project. China has been a significant military supplier to Myanmar and has strategic interests, including a deep sea port at Kyaukphyu. China's investments form 28% of Myanmar's GDP, raising concerns over military use and strategic implications.

Additionally, Chinese companies invest in Myanmar's retail and mobile payment sectors, with Alibaba and Huawei leading in e-commerce and mobile payment platforms.

**Current Civil war in Myanmar:** Myanmar gained independence from Britain in 1948 as a parliamentary democracy. However, in 1964, a military coup led by the Tatmadaw established a military junta with vast constitutional, political, and economic authority. Although the Tatmadaw officially transferred power to a civilian government in 2011, it still retained significant political control and autonomy. In the 2021 elections, following the National League for Democracy's victory, the military executed another coup, forming the State Administration Council (SAC) as Myanmar's government. Subsequently, the ousted National Unity Government (NUG) established the People's Defence Force, leading to the ongoing conflict in Myanmar. The NUG, the primary opposition coalition to the junta, faces heightened violence from various other opposition forces, while the Rohingya crisis in Rakhine State continues without substantial international intervention due to perceived limited gains by Western nations.

Since the military coup in Myanmar, the military's use of artillery and airstrikes has led to the death and injury of numerous civilians, destruction of villages and schools, and the displacement of thousands. The Office of the High Commissioner for Human Rights (OHCHR) reported the destruction of around 30,000 civilian infrastructures, with at least 382 children killed, and other victims subjected to brutal raids, arrests, and extrajudicial killings. More than 16,000 pro-democracy supporters have been arbitrarily arrested, facing allegations of torture and sexual violence during detention. Aung San Suu Kyi, the leader of the ousted National League for Democracy party, has been charged with various offenses, resulting in harsh sentences for her and several of her associates. The situation remains deeply concerning, with ongoing human rights violations in the country.

# -How we can be benefited from this Civil war in Myanmar –

**Step 1 =** The United States should offer Myanmar assistance in resolving the current civil unrest within the country, contingent upon the Myanmar government's willingness to adhere to future instructions provided by the US.

**Step 2 =** A free and fair election, supervised by the U.S, will be held to establish a democratic government in Myanmar. Subsequently, a peace treaty should be forged between Myanmar's newly elected democratic government and the Tatmadaw, stipulating that all civilian departments will fall under the civil government's authority, while matters pertaining to the military, finance, and international affairs will remain under the purview of the Tatmadaw.

**Step 3 =** Moving forward, adhere to instructions provided by the US, Myanmar must cease all bilateral trades with China and refrain from accepting any further financial or military assistance from the country. Additionally, Myanmar shall disallow Chinese investments in its infrastructure projects. Furthermore, when required by the United States, Myanmar will cooperate by granting access to its land & international borders for strategic purposes concerning China.

# -INDIA – CHINA KINETIC WAR-

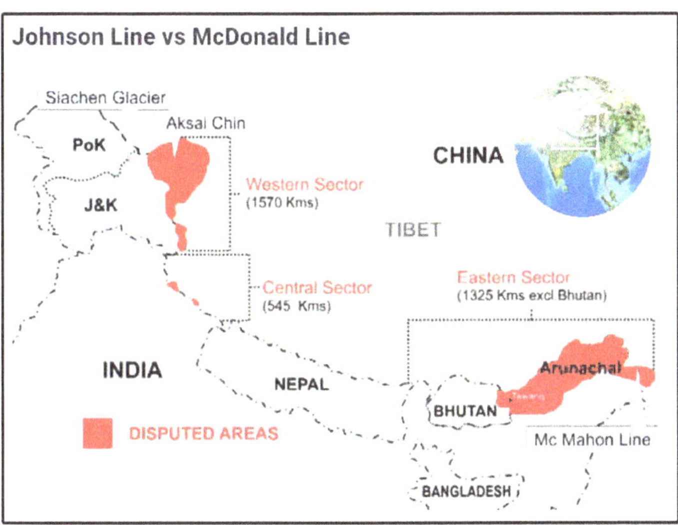


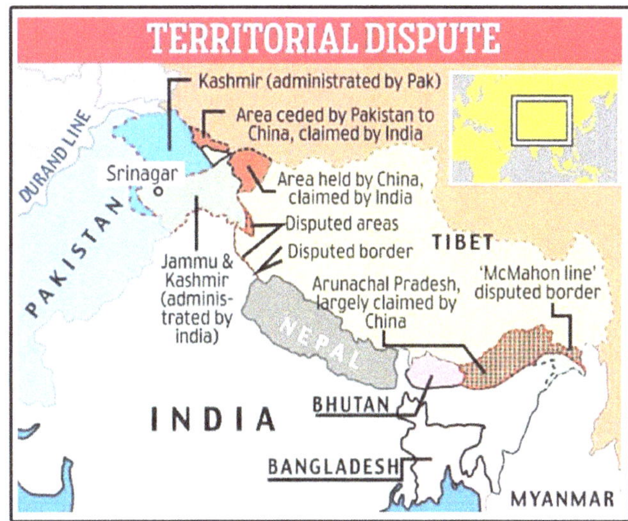


**INDIA - CHINA BORDER DISPUTE**

❖ India VS China full scale active war. (war should be continued atleast more than 2 year long)
- **3 geographic location from where India – China war can be started.**
    - a) *Malacca Strait:* The most important area where Indo-China war can be started. 800km long 60 to 250km wide water area Malaya Penisula & Indonesian island of Sumatra.
    - b) *Askai Chin:* 38000 km, an arid reagion of easternmost Kashmir is claimed by India but currently under Chinese control. Demchok & Chismule Bridge area.
    - c) *Arunachal Pradesh & Dokhlam district of Sikkim:* Since long China claims Arunachal pradesh as part of its Tibet province. And, Dokalm Valley is a very tratigic area for its geographic location. Dokalm is a tri-junction of India-China-Bhutan. China has attempted to construct a road in this location.
- **Why Malacca Strait is so important for China & the world ?**
    - i. *Significance of Malacca Strait:* The Straits of Malacca is one of the most important shipping waterways in the world from both an economic and a strategic perspective. It is

the shortest shipping channel between the Indian Ocean and the Pacific Ocean, linking major economies such as Middle East, China, Japan, South Korea, etc. There are more than 200 vessels passing through the Straits on a daily basis and this gives an annual throughput of approximately 70,000 ships, carrying 80% of the oil transported to Northeast Asia as well as one third of the world's traded goods including Chinese manufactures, Indonesian coffee, etc. (Gilmartin, 2008). Over 400 shipping lines, linking over 700 ports worldwide, regularly utilise the straits for transit and/or transhipment creating one of the world's traffic chokepoints.

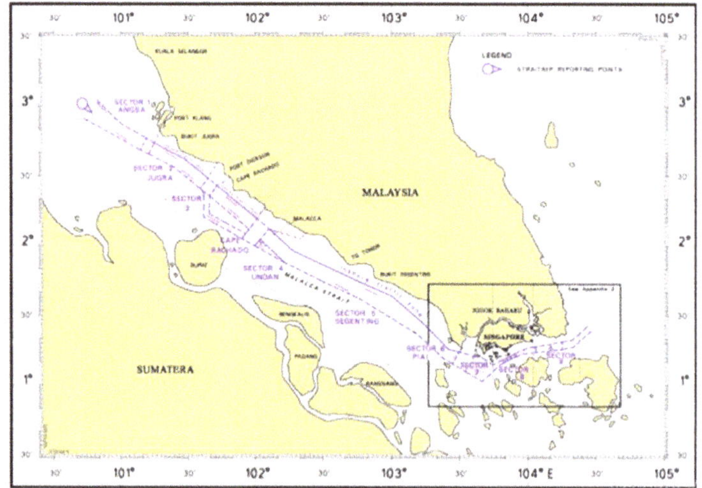


Importance of Malacca strait

ii.  *Indian Armed force:* Andaman and Nicobar Command (ANC) is the first and only tri-service theatre command of the Indian Armed Forces active in Andaman-Nicobar region.

iii. *Target Chanese ships in Malacca strait:* Blocking Malacca strait by Indian Navy will create a huge damage to China. There is no doubt that China will do everything to free this strait from Indian military. India will <u>only target the cargoships which are both import & export goods of China</u> in Malacca starait.

# -INDIA - PAKISTAN WAR-

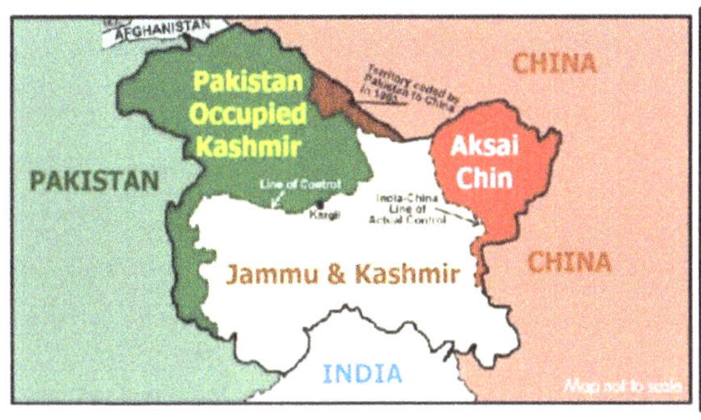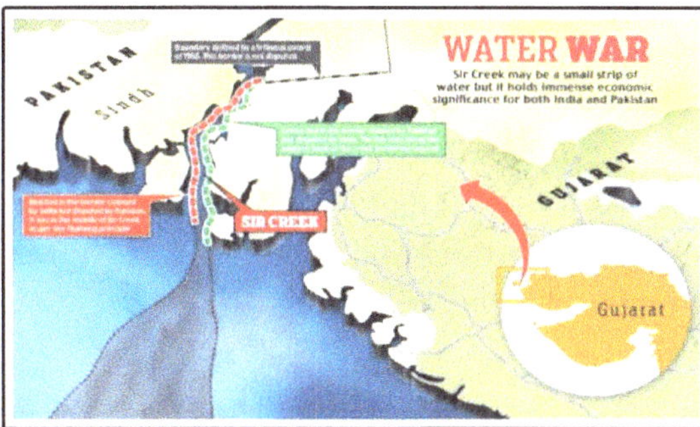

source:https://www.ksgindia.com/

source:https://byjus.com/https://www.ksgindia.com/

**INDIA - PAKISTAN BORDER DISPUTE**

❖ **India VS Pakistan full scale active war.** (war should be continued atleast more than 2 year long)

- *Introduction:* Separated by Redcliff line & later line of control (LOC) Pakistan is a enemy contry of India by birth. Since Long political tension & military operations have been there between these two contries. India & Pakistan, the time has come to ignite the fire. Thus we can make a huge profit from this conflict.
- 3 geographic location from where India – Pakistan war can be started.
    a) *Chiachen Glacier:* 25000 km2 area - a very important high altitutude statigic location for India – Pakistan relation, situated in eastern karakoram range of Himalayas.
    b) *Sir Creek area:* 96 kilometer long strip of water in the marshy land of Rann of Kutch, Gujrat. Sir Creek has crucial economic significance for its oil & gas reservs.
    c) *Kashmir Valley:* the northern part of Srinagar.
- *Pakistan's role:* Pakistan will forcefully invade & capture Indian landmass. Pakistani military will give media interview that, this attack is directly planed & supported by China to damage India.
- *India's role:* India will defense 1st, in 2nd stage India will retaliate with very weak military power. In 3rd stage India will wipe out the Pakistani military. Later stage of this war, India will capture Punjab & Sindh area of Pakistan, & Pakistani military will fight with India to get it's land back.
- *Future of Pakistan:* Break Pakistan into multiple geophaic region. Punjab & sindh will be captured by India. Baluchistan will join Main Afganistan landmass.

# -HOW TO BREAK INDIA-

**Why India is the biggest threat to Western countries:** India is a black horse and has massive potential to become a superpower of not only Asia but also the entire globe. The current BJP government is solely responsible for India's growth in various sectors. It is our primary objective to destroy & break India.

**Here are some key points for this purpose….**

- Remove the CHAIWALA & FAT PIG'S government from power & establish a weak & puppet government in India.
- Engage India in two front wars for a prolonged time- India VS China and India VS Pakistan.
- Economic centralization through the implementation of Digital ID & CBDC wallet to all citizens & Bank consolidation.
- Break India economically.
- Break India's religion & cultural basis.
- Break the education & health care system of India.
- Brainwash Indian people.

## -Remove the CHAIWALA & FAT PIG'S government from power-

**Introduction =** from 2014 onwards the kind of economic growth & political growth India achieved internally & globally under this BJP govt led by Chaiwala is significant. The problem is if we need to fulfill our targets we need to topple his govt & remove the Chaiwala-Fat Pig duet as soon as possible. The bigger problem is, that India has its Loksabha election in mid-2024, & considering the strong position of BJP and Chaiwala, there is an 80% probability that these people will start the third term.

## Here are some suggestions on how we can weaken this govt=

1. **Break RSS:** The BJP's primary influence stems from the RSS (Rashtriya Swayamsevak Sangh). The bedrock of BJP's power lies in the robust foundation provided by RSS. Acting as an incubator, RSS nurtures BJP workers and potential leaders at a national level. RSS serves as the breeding ground where youths evolve into staunch BJP supporters and activists.

It's evolving into a radical Hindu entity that marginalizes other religions, particularly Muslims and Christians in India. It's the mechanism through which the BJP wields soft power over the populace and embodies an ideology of radical Hinduism. Disrupting the RSS could significantly ease other challenges. Apply divide & rule policy among BJP & RSS leaders.

Break RSS internally by firing divergent ideologies among top RSS members. If RSS breaks up into multiple parts led by multiple leaders, it will be much easier for us to form anti-BJP parties on the national level. Bring a sense of insecurity among RSS leaders, every leader is fond of power & prestige. Inveiglete the RSS and BJP leaders for power money prestige.

Modi is too strong to control. This man & Amit Shah have been able to build a strong castle around them, a very strong team of capable ideologically BJP mindset people like- S Jaiskakar, Ajit Doval, J.P Nadda, Rajnath Sing. The hunger for political power, exposure, money & prestige can deceive any man or woman. We have to play some games to internally break them.

2. **Funding to BJP should be stopped:** The BJP is a meticulously organized and well-financed party, where financial prowess stands as a cornerstone for any political success. A significant portion of funding for RSS and BJP stems from affluent businessmen in Gujarat and Rajasthan. Contributions also come from small and medium-scale businessmen in Uttar Pradesh, Himachal Pradesh, Uttarakhand, and Maharashtra. It is imperative to halt this funding.

3. **North-east riots:** Make India's northeast state Manipur riots more violent, & let it spread among 7 sisters (all 7 northeast states of India). Specially Nagaland, Meghalaya & Mizoram. These riots must be turned into a Christianity VS local group intolerance issue because in the northeast these are the Christian majority population oriented. This public insurgency should be on such a large scale that parliament sessions should come to a halt.

4. **BJP minority in South:** Kerala and Maharashtra, particularly in South India, should have representation from the BJP in their minority seats. Southern Indian states hold significant sway in the Indian Parliament. The dominance of any national party thriving in North India and possessing a strong influence in the South illustrates its hegemony over the parliament.

5. **Nationally and internationally Modi should be villainized just like Mr. Putin:** In 2019 BJP passed a "Citizenship law that discriminates Muslims. Most recently BJP BJP-ruled states have passed an anti-conversion law, which is practiced against Muslim men who marry Hindu women. These govt actions violate domestic law and India's obligation under international human rights law (AMNESTY). That prohibits discrimination based on race, ethnicity, or religion. BJP government's actions have stocked communal hatred and created deep fissures in society leading to much fear and mistrust of authorities among minority communities.

6. **Destroy small & medium-sized Businesses:** The small & medium-scale businesses with yearly turnover from 2 cr to 50cr……are mostly run by the traditional family units for 2 or 3 generations. Break this united family system & destroy their business. These people are the main supporters of the BJP govt.

Gujarati and Rajasthani businessman community, specifically the Marwari businessman community runs these family enterprises. They live in a joint family structure, happy marriage with kids & older parent's structure. Break their family system by breaking their marriage. Parents & kids should be separated via… social service freebies like old age-widow pensions. Kids should be separated from their parents via unemployment allowances.

7. **Build mass agitation on NRC & UCC issue:** Creat large public agitation against the govt in NRC (National Register of Citizens) + UCC (Uniform Civil Code) Issue. These issues are mostly vibrant in north-east Indian states & Muslim majority states.

   Sikhs, Muslims, Buddhists, Christians, and Tribal ethnic groups of northeast India.. all these religious groups should fire Anti govt slogans, and ethnic Adivasis and Dalits should also join them.

8. **Re-open Gujrat riot files:** Reopen the files of the Gujrat Riots in the Supreme Court. BJP govt & Modi should be penalized.

9. **Radical Hinduism VS other religious conflicts:** Engage Radical Hindus in RSS with religious conflict with radical Muslims. Practical religious riots should be there at the ground level. Agitate radical Muslim in India. Muslim religious community is the 2nd largest group in India but still lives like a 2nd class citizen. India is the home of more Muslims than Pakistan, Bangladesh, and Afghanistan – the so-called Muslim states.

**We need a weak government in India to practically implement our projects in India.**

**18th Lok Sabha (Lower house of Indian Perlimant) election in April – May:** This will select the 16th Prime Minister of the largest democracy in the world – India.

# -Change in Indian Parliamentary system & Indian constitution-

1. The establishment of a **"Deputy Prime Minister"** role in both chambers of the Indian Parliament is proposed. The selection of this Deputy Prime Minister will be directly overseen by the World Economic Forum (WEF) and the International Monetary Fund (IMF), pending approval from private stakeholders of the Central Bank. This designated official would wield the authority to sanction or invalidate any deliberations within the parliamentary chambers. Any proposition presented to the House Speaker must first secure authorization from the Deputy Prime Minister, thereby granting comprehensive control over parliamentary proceedings, protocols, discussions, and deliberations.

2. **The formation of the New Central Bank of India** as a private entity necessitates constitutional amendments.

3. Constitutional support is imperative for advocating divorce and LGBT rights.

4. Procedural changes in both houses, namely Lok Sabha and Rajya Sabha, are imperative.

5. There's a proposal to annul all other political parties except our own, aiming to ensure prolonged governance by a single party in the government.

6. **Shift the Capital of India from New Delhi to Kolkata:** By the move the influence of north Indian businessman on Indian perliament & government policies will be reduced.

# -Break India economically-

India, with its vast population of 1.5 billion people and diverse economic and social strata, faces the challenge of continuing as a net importer of finished goods, perpetuating the perception of Indian labor as inexpensive despite the acknowledged international efficiency of its workforce. To achieve significant control over economic policies, there's a need to influence both central and state government policies directly or indirectly, shaping the nation's economic trajectory.

*Key strategies to undermine the Indian economy include:*

## Economic Colonisation through change the Central banking system of India & Bank consolidation:

1. The Central Bank of India – Reserve Bank should be a private entity with shareholders. There will be a board consisting share shareholders & the governor & deputy Governor.
2. Governor & deputy governors & executives will be selected directly by the shareholders. Government employees like civil servants, auditors, accountants, technical analysts, managers, and clerks will be appointed by the government.
3. In the central parliament, a special team of Monetary policy will be appointed by the private shareholders. This committee will have the power to approve or nullify any monetary policy taken by the central legislators. Thus indirectly we will have control over the monetary policy of the government.
4. There should be no match between monetary policy & fiscal policy in parliament.
5. This new central bank of India will be empowered with unlimited credit creation capacity. Thus India will be sunk into perpetual indebtedness.
6. A vast pool of data & information of bank customers will be managed by a private company through blockchain technology, whose ownership will be held by private players who also own the shares of Central Bank. Customer data-tokenization of financial assets of the bank customers etc... will be provided by this private company to the central bank. Thus Digital ID & CBDC can be practically implemented.

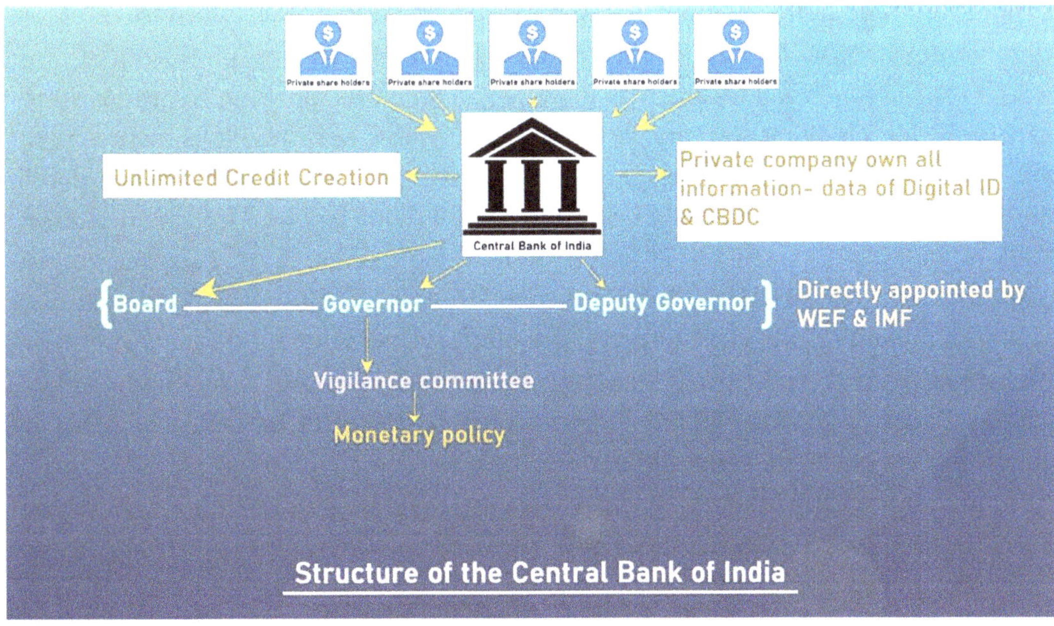

- **Bank consolidation:** We don't need many banks in India. There are 12 public sector banks and some private banks in India. Small banks must be consolidated with larger banks & all customer data must be centralized to a private company which is directly under the supervision on a newly modified private central bank.
- **Increase Deficit Spending:** Advocating for government spending to surpass earnings significantly.
- **Engagement in Active Wars:** Proposing active involvement in prolonged Indo-China and Indo-Pak wars to drain resources and facilitate investment opportunities post-war.
- **Currency Debasement:** Diminishing the international purchasing power of the Indian currency.
- **Direct Control of Banking, Insurance, and Stock Markets:** Seeking complete control over these sectors to manipulate economic activities.
- **Implementation of Welfare Schemes:** Fostering a culture of welfare dependency, offering pensions, allowances, and loans to discourage a productive working culture.
- **Control over Infrastructure and Capital Assets:** Seeking control over all critical assets, from railways and power plants to lands and natural resources.
- **Tax Reforms:** Advocating for increased tax brackets to cover a significant portion of the population, thus reducing disposable income across society.
- Moreover, proposed steps include implementing taxes on life events like birth, death, and marriage, charging insurance fees for travel, curbing evasion of capital gains tax,
- **Carbon Credit Score:** A carbon credit score on a family should be applied. How much fossil fuel that family is using per month should be tracked & on that amount, a credit score should be assigned. The use of fossil fuel & carbon credit score is in reverse relation. More the use of fossil fuel less the credit score. In addition, if the family is using any form of green energy their carbon credit score will increase. Based on that carbon credit score tax will be applied to them. This Carbon credit score will be linked with their Digital ID.
- **Physical Cashless Economy:** Moving towards a cashless society, at least 80% cashless by 2030.
- **High Trade deficit:** India should be a net exporter of goods & services but all medium & large companies will be owned by us. So, We will have financial gain at the expense of India's resources. The more the trade deficit in the current account more the financial burden.
- **Heavy investment in green energy:** Fulfilling the target of SDG-2030- reducing carbon footprint. These funds will be given as loans. India aims to transition to green energy, emphasizing electric vehicles, charging stations, and FDI in renewable sectors. Plans involve privatizing thermal plants, doubling renewable energy targets, and leveraging the International Solar Alliance's initiatives for solar power. Seeking IMF funds, India plans to boost its green energy infrastructure, inviting foreign energy companies into its market.
- **Promotion of the private sector in the finance industry:** Banking & asset management companies, private insurance regulators, like black rock & others.
- **Promotion of AI & machine learning:** In manufacturing units & assembling hubs use of modern machines, robots, and Artificial intelligence-machine. Human labor must be replaced by machines. So, unemployment can be generated.
- **Destroy the middle-income group:** This strategy aims to destabilize the middle class, which forms the backbone of India's economy and society, intending to create a societal structure

composed solely of an elite class and labor force serving the elite, ultimately eradicating the middle-income group and its economic, social, and cultural impact on the nation.



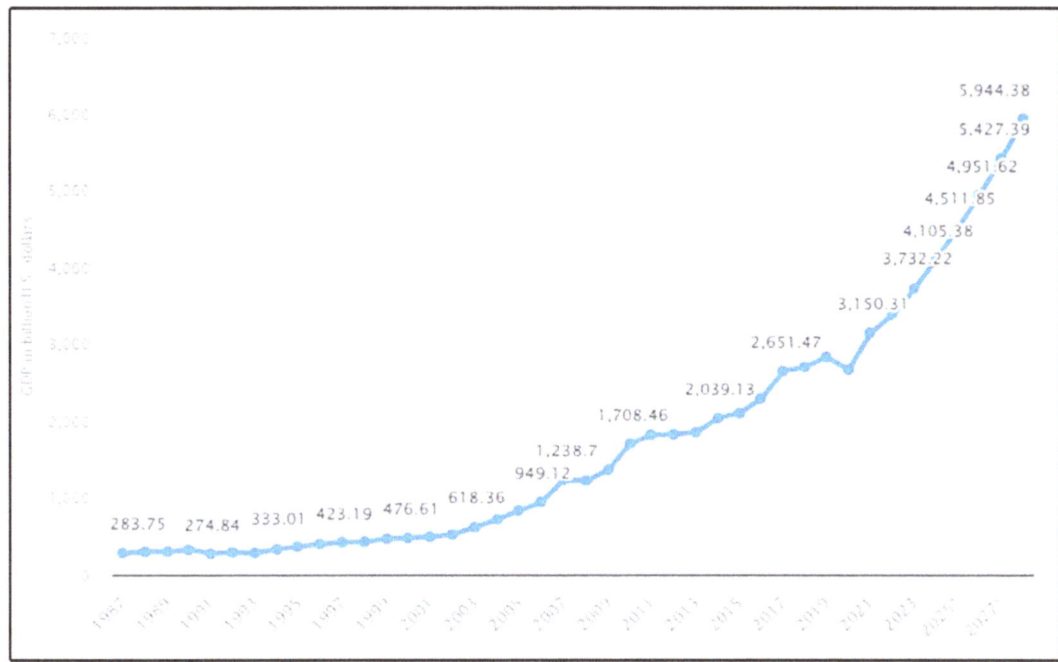

source: https://www.statista.com/ **India – GDP growth from 1987 to 2027**

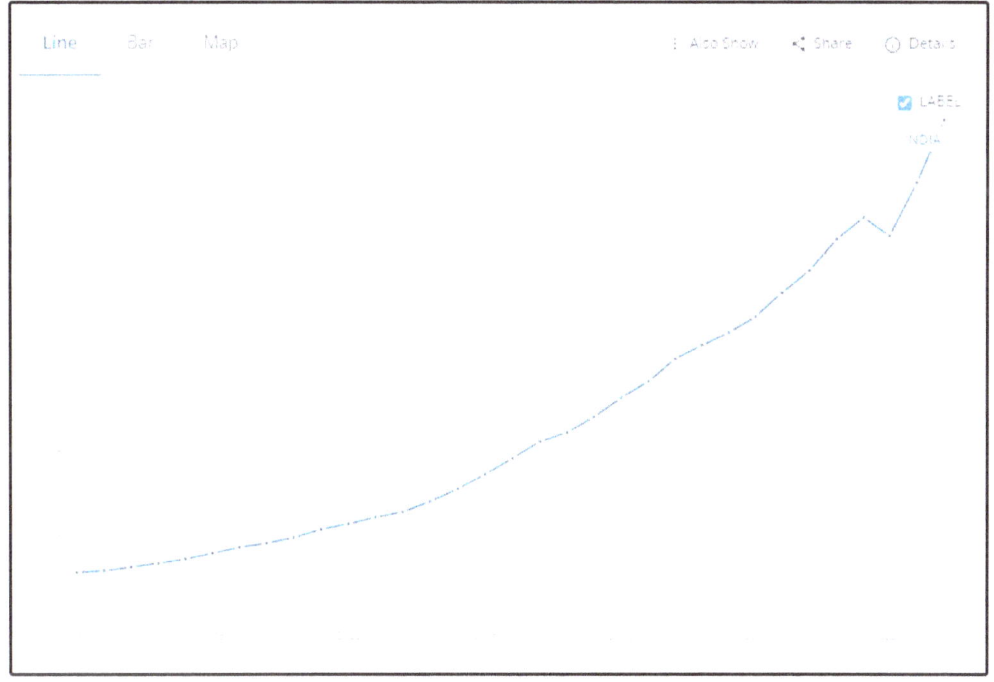

**India – GDP.PPP (current international $)**
source: https://data.worldbank.org/

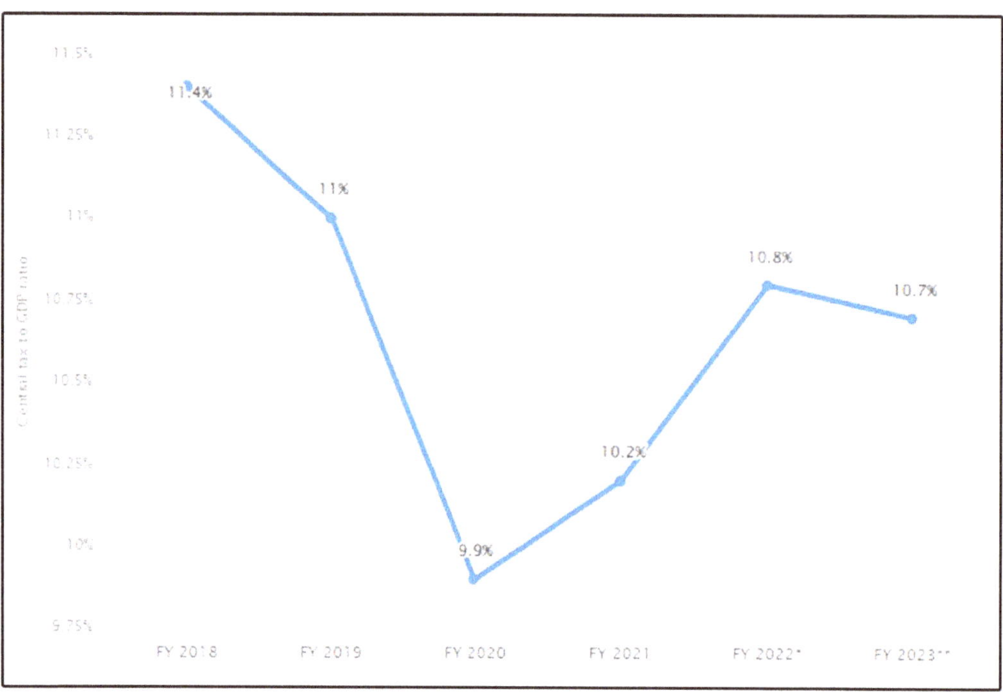



source: https://www.statista.com/

# -Break India religion & cultural basis-

**Introduction =** India has had a long history of communal violence since independence. Though the Preamble of the Constitution asserted that India is a secular nation, after independence more than 100 large & small communal violence had taken place. India being a cocktail of religious dogma it has been very easy to fire any communal violence based on religious beliefs & make a profit out of it. Making Indian people more intolerant in religious matters & engaging them in chaos is our primary goal.

**The preamble of the Indian constitution says:** India aims to stand as a sovereign, socialist, secular, and democratic republic. Secularism, in this context, signifies a stance of indifference towards, rejection of, or exclusion from religious considerations. It ensures liberty and equality for all citizens while fostering fraternity to preserve the unity and integrity of the nation.

Fundamental rights are asserted to the Indian people in the Indian constitution.

**Article 14 =** equality before law,

**Article 15 =** Prohibition of discrimination.

**Article 16 =** equal opportunity in public employment.

**Article 17 =** Abolition of untouchability.

**Articles 26-30** of the constitution grant freedom of religion as a fundamental right.

As per Pew Research On the question of inter-religious marriage, most Hindus (67%), Muslims (80%), Sikhs (59%), and Jains (66%) felt it was 'very important' to stop the women in their community from marrying outside their religion.

## Reasons behind religious & communal intolerance in India:

- **Political history:** Since the medieval age India was the home of multi-ethnic groups. From time to time Hindus, Muslims, Europeans, and local tribal groups used to fight for political & economic power.
- **Conflict of Interests:** Communal conflicts are a means for communities to assert their communal identities and to demand their share in economic, educational, and job opportunities. Especially in the present times of economic downturn.
- **Resource Crunch:** India holds the largest population on this planet but has only 2% of the land mass of the world. With an exponentially growing population, people are fighting for the ownership of limited natural resources like land, water, minerals, etc.
- **Threat to minority:** A rise in intolerance and communal disharmony leads to majoritarianism and thus, suppresses minorities and hinders their rights.
- **Regionalism:** The anti-national elements get adequate opportunity to fan regional feelings and work on creating an atmosphere to break the cohesiveness of our society.
- **Vote Bank Politics:** The politicians use the communal card to align themselves to a particular community or to break up the vote bank of another party often indulging in instigating a communal riot.
- **Rise of the pro-Hindu Bharatiya Janata Party:** political shift as a mandate to advance the movement toward a Hindu-only nation.
- **Even though Hindus form close to 80 percent of the population, India also has region-specific religious practices:** for instance, Jammu and Kashmir has a Muslim majority, Punjab has a Sikh majority, Nagaland, Meghalaya, and Mizoram have Christian majorities and the Indian Himalayan States such as Sikkim and Ladakh, Arunachal Pradesh and the state of Maharashtra and the Darjeeling District of West Bengal have large concentrations of Buddhist population.
- The country has significant Muslim, Sikh, Christian, Buddhist, Jain, and Zoroastrian populations.
- Islam is the largest minority religion in India, and Indian Muslims form the third largest Muslim population in the world, accounting for over 14 percent of the nation's population.

## Most violent communal riots in recent years:

- **2002 Gujarat riots:** On February 27, 2002, a suspected Muslim mob attacked a train carrying activists of the Vishwa Hindu Parishad (VHP) back from the disputed holy site of Ayodhya. The attack left 58 Hindu activists dead.
- **1992 Mumbai riots:** Hours after the demolition of the Babri masjid, Mumbai erupted. For five days in December 1992 and then again for a fortnight in January, the city witnessed unprecedented riots. As many as 1,788 people were killed and property worth crores of rupees was destroyed.
- **1989 Bhagalpur riots:** On October 23, 1989, began the month-long riots triggered by police atrocities. saw massacre and arson in which over 1,000 people died, nearly 50,000 were displaced and 11,500 houses were torched.

- **The Anti-Sikh Riots of 1984**: started after Indira Gandhi, the then Prime Minister of India was assassinated by her Sikh bodyguards. This led to a huge amount of chaos and bloodshed in Delhi as well as other parts of India and most of the violence was directed against the Sikhs. Almost 2800-3000 people died in the riots and nearly 2100 of these people died in Delhi itself.
- **The Bhagalpur Riots of 1989**: Regarded as one of the worst massacres in India. The main reason for the riots was an attack on Hindus and the subsequent killing of two Hindu men by a reportedly Muslim group. October month reason - Religious procession and false rumors about the killing of Hindu students. Death of 1000+ people.
- **Kashmir Riots 1989:** Ever since Independence, Kashmir has been plagued by consistent operations launched by the insurgents. However, things took an ugly turn with the riots of 1989 when the majority of Muslims made every possible attempt to evacuate Hindus from Jammu and Kashmir. Anantnag in southern Kashmir was at the center of all the controversy. A lot of Kashmiri pundits lost their homes as a result of the communal crime.
- **The Aligarh Riots of 2006**: On 5 April. It was Ram Navami. The riots happened because of an alleged misunderstanding between Hindus and Muslims. Almost 6 people died and many were injured. Soon after the incident, authorities imposed a curfew, helping the region become normal once again.
- **2020 Delhi riots:** february-march - CAA-NRC Protests- Muslims, Hindu

## How Religious inequality can be increased among Indian people:

1. **Starting Madrassa schools for Muslims:** Based on religious beliefs the Madrassa schooling system can give birth to hatred emotion among Muslim kids towards other non-muslim communities. These kids after 10-20 years will be the propagator of hate & violence.
2. Integrate extremism beliefs in public education. In school textbooks, chapters will be given to develop religious intolerance. In college radical religious community must be formed.
3. Ethnic groups & minority religion community should be given privilege in various government schemes & employments.
4. **Dedicated groups in various Social media platforms and dedicated Media TV channels for a particular religious group:** people of that particular religion can be united & promoted hatred – violence, false propaganda, false news of supprecession, and tyranny by the other religious group.
5. State governments will ban certain religious festivals in a particular state in the context of environmental pollution, and animal rights so that particular religious groups will agitate against the government.
6. Muslims -Being the 2nd largest religious community in India.. in 80 years of post-independence – " Why India can't have a Muslim PM." This should be in the anti-govt agenda.

# -Inter – state river water sharing dispute-

**Introduction:** India is a land of rivers. 100s of small & large river India is flowing & since the ancient time these rivers are time center of human civilization development. In modern days there are several ongoing conflicts among Indian states for the share of river water. This conflict is very important for inciting intolerance & radicalism among people. People in India depend on the river from multiple angles, including their economic & cultural activities.



This is a purely research & planning based highly confidential document created by Shyam Sundar Saha.
Mail id: Shyamsaha7@gmail.com, mobile no & whats app +91 9239538327, Kolkata, India.

- **Art 246 deals with the 7th schedule** of the Indian constitution consisting of 3 individual lists, a state list, a center list & conconrent list markets the topic that only the state only centergovbnemnt & can apply their powers.
- **Entry 17** in the state list deals with water i.e. water supply, irrigation, canal, drainage, embankments, water storage, and water power.
- **Entry 56 of the Union List empowers** the Union Government for the regulation and development of inter-state rivers and river valleys to the extent declared by Parliament to be expedient in the public interest.

## According to Article 262, in case of disputes relating to waters:
- Parliament may by law provide for the adjudication of any dispute or complaint concerning the use, distribution, or control of the waters of, or in, any inter-State river or river valley.
- Parliament may, by law provide that neither the Supreme Court nor any other court shall exercise jurisdiction in respect of any such dispute or complaint as mentioned above.

## Major inter-state river disputes =
- Narmada – Madhya Pradesh, Gujrat, Maharastra, Rajasthan.
- Krishna – Maharashtra, Andhra Pradesh, Karnataka, Telangana,
- Godavari – Maharastra, Andhra Pradesh, Karnataka, Madhya Pradesh, Odisha.
- Cauvery – Kerala, Karnataka, Tamil Nadu, Puducherry.
- There are various Active River Water Dispute Tribunals in India.

# -Break India in social basis-

Family is the base of a strong social structure. From the ancient and medieval eras Indians irrespective of their religion, believed in a joint-family structure. In a joint-family structure, 8 to 15 people (3 generations) stay together sharing their daily needs from food to washroom. In this model, any person in the family feels more secure in terms of financial status, health emergency, or any other bad events that took place in the family.

But, to make a profit out of capitalism, this joint family structure had to be broken. Due to the globalization & opening of the Indian market to foreign companies by LPG (liberalization, privatization, and globalization) reforms in 1991, this joint-family structure has been broken successfully and leads to a new era of nuclear family structure where husband-wife with one or two children live together.

Now our primary task is, to break down the rest % of the joint-family structure & the nuclear family structure of India. This is how the capitalist economy makes a profit out of this broken family system….

1. The more one person lives alone out of his/her family the more goods & commodities are needed to survive the daily lifestyle.
2. Men & women both compete in the same job market, so capitalists will have access to a cheaper labor force.
3. By living an individual lifestyle physical inequality increases, which demands more social service schemes from the government, resulting in more deficit spending to the government. The government has to

borrow more & more money to run the social service schemes. This increases the national debt of a country.



## ⌐ To break the family system in India, we have to promote the following campaigns:

1. Individualism:
2. Feminism & Women Empowerment:
3. Ultra-urban lifestyle.
4. Pre-marital sex and extramarital affairs, divorce
5. An unmarried individual man or woman can adopt & raise children.
6. Promotion of Government social service schemes, like- old age pension to all, Unemployment allowance, divorced women get an allowance, medical allowance, widow allowance..etc.

India is a Hindu-majority country. In the last nine years under the Modi government, the Hindu Sanatan dharma proliferated in all aspects. Specifically in north Indian states the practice of religious rituals has been growing significantly. This also helps a great profit-making business model for the small & medium businessmen who are involved in the commercialization of Hindu Sanatan dharma.

Another religious majority group, the Muslims also play a very rooted ideology in its religious ideology. India has been always rich in its multi-dimensional culture. But with access to Western ideology & the internet & English education the core inheritance beliefs, rituals, and ideology have been fading out. This is a situation of complete mocktail where a single person is confused about what is best practice for him or her. This is the right time to employ them in Western culture & ideology.

**Our primary motive** is to uproot Indian people from their own culture & social values & brainwash them to destroy.

## Here are some key points to achieve this:

**Destruct Hindu Sanatan dhrama:** Modi-BJP-RSS are the pros of this. Indian people should believe & practice their religion.
Radial ideology in a particular religious group must be developed. This will help in increasing internal conflicts among people. Muslim women should be highly educated & economically empowered.

**Break the family system:** Kids should be separated from their parents, parents don't need kids because they will be given old age pensions. Kids don't need parents because they will be under the state welfare system (allowance).

**Increase the rate of Divorce:** The legal process for divorce ought to be so simplified that both getting married and obtaining a divorce become as effortless as child's play. Two to three times divorced women should be promoted in media, and news – this will be an inspiration for millions, that to protect their freedom & self-dignity women never sacrifice.

**Increase free sex, pre-marital sex, and extra-marital affairs:** Sex is the most powerful pleasure hormone in the human brain. Lust and perversion must be promoted. Clubs must be organized where free sex-alcohol-drugs are easily available. Both men and women should be empowered to choose his or her sexual partner, or emotional partner outside of their married relationship. This should be legalized through constitutional backing in the name of fundamental rights, human dignity, and personal freedom. Pornography & sex services must be promoted.

**Promote the LGBT community:** They should be given the right to live in their way. We should create some models for the masses so they can be inspired. They should be given media highlights and promotions. They can be used in political campaigns to gain support.

**Women empowerment:** The woman of a family is the main strong force to binds the family unit. In modern life where women also go for jobs it not only destroys the social structure but also breaks the family. To break the family system women should be given limited less freedom with arrogance & money. From the very beginning a mental state - an ideology should be built up in women that women don't need men to live a healthy & secure life. This will increase the unmarried population & free sex.

**A great combination of Rock & roll music with Drugs:** Pop music singers, and bands must be promoted. Young stars must be crazy to watch their favorite musical hero, bands. Live performances of them will drive the young people crazy. Music videos- albums must be produced where rock & roll music- rap – western music will be picturized with semi-nude women, bikinis, and onscreen perversions. This will be combined with the wave of new ideas- modern philosophy, drugs, heroin, LSD. Night clubs must be there in every metropolitan city where free sex- pop music- and drugs are easily available.

**Open the Flood gate of Immigration:** From Bangladesh, Pakistan, Vietnam, and China, -- massive immigrants must enter India. This will degrade the cultural & social quality of India. This immigrant population will be a cheap source of human labor.

**Social media platforms & TV channels:** Social media platforms and television channels play a crucial role in the degradation of culture. These platforms immerse people in a virtual world, with Facebook, Instagram, TikTok, and YouTube successfully capturing a significant part of daily life. While daily soap serials aim to showcase women's empowerment, they often inadvertently promote family discord, jealousy, and hostility, leading to the breakdown of family units.

**Fashion industry =** Chennai, Delhi, Mumbai, Bangalore, Surat, Ammdabad – are the top fashion hubs in India. In addition, these cities are also metropolitan cities having modern lifestyles. What we have to do is, we must introduce an ultra-modern vulgar lifestyle.

**Promote the Modeling industry (showing woman's body):** Genetically all men have been addicted to sex & food from ancient times. So, it will be much easier for us to engage the human mind in food & sexual activities all day.

Semi-nude fashion show – ramp walk must be organized in these cities. The modeling industry is an attractive industry for women to be glamorous, get easy money & quick fame. All colleges should be fashion shows on an annual completion basis, so it will be easy for us the pick the best talent. We have to include glamour & fashion & sports in the college education system in such a way that the focus of the youngsters will be easily shifted from studies to these things.

**Women's sports in bikinis:** Showing women's bodies and attracting people's attention is our motif. Sorts like beach volleyball, football, rugby, atlites, cross-fit championships, and diving must be promoted. Advertise them.

# -Break the education of India-

**Introduction:** Education molds individuals, much like how people form the backbone of a nation's stature. Across nations, education stands as a foundational pillar, nurturing knowledge, ethics, and consciousness, while also driving technological progress.

**In India** "Education" is a concurrent subject listed in the 7th schedule which means both the Parliament and the State Legislatures can make laws in Education.

## Constitutional provisions:

- Part IV of the Indian Constitution, Article 45, and Article 39 (f) of Directive Principles of State Policy (DPSP) have a provision for state-funded as well as equitable and accessible education.
- The 42nd Amendment to the Constitution in 1976 moved education from the State to the Concurrent List.
- The 86th Amendment in 2002 made education an enforceable right under Article 21-A.
- The right to education is a fundamental right to Indian citizens enacted in Art 21 (A).
- **Article 350 A directs, "It shall he endeavor of every state and every local authority to provide adequate facilities for instruction in the mother-tongue at the primary stage of education to children belonging to linguistic minority groups."**
- **Art 46 - Promotion of education and economic interests of SC, ST, and other weaker sections.**

## Our objective:

- The primary objective is, to break the Indian education system so that in the future Indian people will not be able to fit into the formal job sector & incompetent in any field.
- **A self-destructive education system must be applied to Indian people. Through this, we will destroy their family values and culture. After finishing graduation or higher studies there will be no match between what they have studied & the practical demands of any formal job.**
- Prepare a multilayered labor class people where every type of labor will be available from manual jobs to intellectual level. So fierce completion best-talented labor will be produced. The best talent at a cheap price will be easily available.
- To prepare a small percentage of highly educated, smart & intelligent & skilled labor force, which can be used by foreign companies to run business in India & globally. As we all know Indian labour is pretty cheap & very skilled & efficient.

- ➤ **Recently Indian parliament announced the "National Education Policy 2020" (5 + 3 + 3 + 4) programme.**

- ➤ **A pupil should invest as many years as possible in this self-destructive education system:** By this policy when a student passes the 12th standard he or she will be at least 18 years old, & 15 years of his or her life has been invested in education.

- After this college degree in a general stream or any specialized stream make it a five years course.
- **A policy should be taken where a higher education (post-graduation) degree will be a dream for every middle-class & lower middle-class family.** And a pupil will invest at least 23 years of his life in this rat race where numbers & gradation will be the ultimate criteria for success not the quality of education, not the quality of knowledge they acquire in this faze.
- **Promotion of Regional language in the Education system:** Regional language or mother tongue should be the medium of education till graduation. And English as a subject should be removed from the course curriculum till graduation. Thus after investing 23-24 years of life in this education system, a person will not be able to compete with the higher class English student in the job market. **English as a** language should be taught only in private schools where economically strong families can afford to admit their children. Thus we can create an upper-class English-speaking Western mindset labour force.
- **Regional language medium in school education & English language medium in Higher education:** All post-graduation higher education courses, like Ph.D.s, M-Phills, and Doctorets should be in English medium. Even in all higher education courses er entrance exams, government competitive exams should be in the English language, thus pupils from studied from a regional language will not be able to compete in job competitions.

## ¬How the syllabus should be given:

- Focus more & more on trivial matters, factual data that changes every year. So pupils will be busy the entire year just mugging up the trivial facts.
- Remove concepts, and understanding type topics.
- They should be devoid of critical thinking, reasoning ability, decision-making process, analytical capability, problem problem-solving approach.
- The weightage of science subjects' mathematics, Physics, and chemistry – should be significantly down. So science mentality will not be developed among them.
- Literature subjects and the history of their regional languages should be taught in a very vast manner.
- In exam MCQ types questions in science subjects, where mugging up trivial facts will be the only way out to score high.
- For literature subjects Long answers should asked in the exam, where students will be provided study notes from the school & to score high in literature they must mug up those long paragraphs.
- Indian people should be uprooted from their own culture & history. So, Indian geography, Indian history, and Indian Science should be removed from the syllabus. The great Indian freedom struggle in modern India must be removed.
- They will be told that Western culture, western history, and Western geography are far better than their Indian history.
- Design the syllabus & curriculum in such a way, the style of pedagogy in such a way that from an early age, students develop attention deficit hyperactivity disorder (ADHD) hoye jay. They lose their focusing ability.
- They will be told that if Europeans and Western powers had not come to India, India would have been so uncivilized, too much underdeveloped. It was the Europeans and Western powers who made India developed.
- All famous Indian personalities (Vivekananda, Gandhi, Vallabhai Patel..etc) must be removed from the syllabus & European personalities should be included in the syllabus.

## Exam pattern:

- From class 8 to 12, students should be given two chances to pass in the final exam. If a student fails in the final year exam he or she will be given another chance after 3 months to re-write those failed subjects.
- In science subjects only MCQ types questions based on trivial matter & in literature subjects answer types questions based on paragraph formats will be given in the exam pattern.

## Mid-day meal system & other facilities are given in school.

- ✓ Our primary moto is to increase the social service expenditure on the government, so this will lead to deficit spending.
- ✓ Our primary objective is to make Indian people ideal, easy food available in the schools, easy pensions, allowances, and dopamine of easy money to the public.
- ✓ In the Indian schooling system, from class 1 to class 8 all government, semi-government schools will provide mid-day meals to their student. Cooked lunch will be served to the students.
- ✓ From class 9 to class 12 students will be provided cash allowances instead of cooked food. By-cycle, school dress, school bag, books, and copies will be provided.
- ✓ In class 9 they will be provided "Tablet" with internet connections.

## Brainwash students with soft power- films, videos, documentaries.

- Every school in India irrespective of government or private must have a projection system. Where a list of selected films, videos, interviews, documentaries, and advertisements will be screened.
- Through these video projections….we will inject misinformation into the brains of the students. Our primary objective is to build radical Hindus, radical Muslims, anti-India sentiments, and religious intolerance. So that, in future it will be quite easy to fan the flames.

## Build radical Hindu Ideology & radical Muslim Ideology through the schooling system.

- ➢ For Hindus, their Gods, religious beliefs, and cultures should be projected as far superior to Muslims.
- ➢ For Muslims to start – the Madrasa schooling system will be implemented where only radical Muslim ideology will be nourished based on religious scriptures.

## Allowances, and scholarships given to school students:

- To receive a direct cash allowance a student & his parents must have a Digital ID and CBDC wallet.
- This allowance will be transferred to their CBDC wallet as a digital currency.

## Behind this allowance, our main target is- Habituate Indian people with the dopamine of easy money allowance.

- ❖ All students irrespective of gender will receive digital money while admitted in class 5.
- ❖ Every year from class 9 to class 12 a passed student will receive digital money into his CBDC wallet.
- ❖ On passing the graduation & post-graduation he will receive digital money into his CBDC wallet.
- ❖ In classes 10, and 12, graduation, and post-graduation meritorious students will be awarded certificates and digital money as scholarships.

**Sports and Practical note bookmaking must be an integral part of the new syllabus.**

In higher Education- Innovation, research & developments, all these aspects of progress must be devoid from the course curriculum.

# -How to break the Health sector of India-

- In India, 80% of the healthcare system is aiming to increase its investment in digital healthcare tools in the coming five years.
- The healthcare industry comprises – hospitals, media devices, clinical trials, outsourcing, telemedicine, medical tourism, health insurance.. etc.
- Indian healthcare delivery system is categorized into two major components: public & private.
- The government (public healthcare system) comprises limited secondary and tertiary care institutions and focuses on providing basic healthcare facilities in the form of primary healthcare centers (PHC) in rural areas.
- The private sector provides a majority of secondary, tertiary, and quaternary care institutions with major concentration in metro cities, tire 1 and tire 2 cities.
- The economic survey of 2022 (the most authentic government report) says: that India's public expenditure on healthcare stood at 2.1 % of GDP in 2021-22. Against 1.8% in 2020-21 and 1.3% in 2019-20.==== era graph e dekhau.
- The Indian medical tourism market was valued at $ 2.89 billion in 2020 and is expected to reach $ 13.42 billion by 2026.

## Problems in India's healthcare sector:

1. Inadequate access to basic healthcare facilities such as a shortage of medical professionals. The current doctor-to-patient ratio in India is 1:834 against the WHO norms of 1:1,000. India still lags far behind the other Asian countries.
2. **Lack of quality assurance,**
3. **Insufficient health spending.**
4. **Infrastructure constraints:**
5. **The strong role of private players.**
6. **Poor insurance penetration:**
7. **Numerous Government Schemes and its limitations:**

## National Health Mission (NHM) a central govt policy launched in 2013:

- Health system strengthening in rural and urban areas for Reproductive maternal–natal chain and adolescent Health (RMNCA) and communicable and non-communicable Diseases.
- **NHM a**lso provides provisions of a range of free services related to maternal Health, Child Health, Adolescent Health, family planning, Universal immunization programs, Tuberculosis, and other vector-borne disease like Malaria, Dengu, Kala Azar, Leporxy etc….

· The Indian healthcare sector demands huge infrastructure support for foreign aid in the form of loans and private investors should come to meet the demand.

· A national health card should be there to track all diseases and treatments a person / his family members get. This needs a big data pool to track all the medical activities of a person. EK Bharat ek health card, One nation one health card.

· An insurance plan must be linked with the National health card so health insurance premiums can be collected according to the income brackets.

· Under this health card Indian citizen will be divided into 4 categories respective to their income. They will get government benefits & subsidies according to the card category. Health insurance will be linked with this card type.

· A strong strong network should be made by private companies for diagnosis, treatment, medicines, and surgeries…. Bill will be generated as they want as high possible, govt will pay a % of that bill as a subsidy.

# -CHINA-

To counter China's strategy, a strategic plan involves the gradual disengagement of the Chinese economy over the next 10 to 20 years. This entails relocating manufacturing and production hubs from China to countries such as India, Bangladesh, Vietnam, Cambodia, Africa, and Pakistan. However, this transition is lengthy and demands meticulous preparation. Before commencing the disengagement, it's imperative to assert control over the economies of these nations set to replace Chinese manufacturing hubs. This includes overseeing their energy resources, natural reserves, minerals, labor markets, infrastructure, currency, foreign reserves, and more. Consequently, some advocate that initiating a conflict akin to World War 3 may be the only solution to execute this strategy effectively.

The trade discord between the United States and China, initially sparked by China's alleged unfair economic policies, has transformed into a broader confrontation characterized as a cold war rooted in conflicting ideologies. Tensions escalated sharply in 2018 when President Donald Trump's concerns about trade deficits prompted the imposition of punitive tariffs on Chinese imports. This action was followed by restrictions on China's access to high-tech US goods and investments, with accusations of unfair commercial practices further exacerbating the rift.

Allegations of China's failure to safeguard intellectual property rights, particularly technology theft, have been the subject of intense debate. While China stands accused of pilfering foreign intellectual property, particularly in technology, a comprehensive analysis suggests that such incidents might not be as frequent or exaggerated once the scale of China's foreign transactions and research activities are considered.

Trade wars are commonly viewed as byproducts of protectionism, where governments enact measures to shield domestic industries and jobs from foreign competition. The surge in trade between the US and China, evidenced by the increase in US imports from China from approximately $100 billion in 2001 to $500 billion in 2021, underscores China's pivotal role in global supply chains. This surge is facilitated by Chinese factories assembling products using components sourced globally for export to the US.

Moreover, increased trade with China was found to boost the average purchasing power of US households by $1,500 between 2000 and 2007, according to a 2019 study by economists Xavier Jaravel and Erick Sager. However, concerns about national security have mounted in the US, especially regarding Chinese attempts to acquire sensitive technology, potentially impacting US industrial policies and military capabilities.

China's strategic subsidization of industries to create "national champion" companies and its ambitious "Made in China 2025" policy, aimed at asserting dominance in global high-tech manufacturing, have raised eyebrows nternationally. This ten-year program seeks to revamp China's manufacturing base by rapidly advancing ten high-tech sectors, including electric vehicles, next-gen IT, robotics, and artificial intelligence. The overarching objective is to transition China's economy away from resource-heavy and low-value sectors towards a high-tech, high-productivity model, aiming to surpass Western technological prowess.

The consequences of the US-China trade war have been significant, impacting the American economy without resolving the underlying economic concerns it was meant to address. There's been a tangible impact on US manufacturing jobs and intellectual property due to what's perceived as unfair Chinese trade practices, including forced technology transfer, limited market access, IP theft, and state-backed subsidies to enterprises.

Heather Long's analysis in the Washington Post highlighted the adverse effects of the trade war, citing slowed economic growth, frozen business investments, increased bankruptcies among farmers, and downturns in manufacturing and freight transportation sectors, comparable to the lows seen in previous recessions. The actions taken during this period have been likened to one of the largest tax increases in years, significantly affecting various sectors of the American economy.

# -ECONOMIC POLICY of CHINA-

In 2020, China's estimated GDP stood at $14.9 trillion according to current market exchange rates, with a real GDP growth of approximately 1.9%. The nation's population reached 1.4 billion, sourced from the IMF.

Trade between the United States and China amounted to an estimated $615.2 billion in 2020. This included $164.9 billion in exports from the US to China and $450.4 billion in imports from China, resulting in a trade deficit of $285.5 billion for the US in 2020.

China ranked as the third-largest goods export market for the United States in 2020. US goods exports to China totaled $124.5 billion, with top export categories including electrical machinery ($17 billion), soybeans ($15 billion), machinery ($14 billion), mineral fuels ($10.0 billion), and optical and medical instruments ($9.5 billion).

Conversely, China emerged as the largest supplier of goods imports for the United States in 2020. US goods imports from China reached $434.7 billion, with primary import categories encompassing electrical machinery ($111 billion), machinery ($97 billion), toys and sports equipment ($26 billion), furniture and bedding ($23 billion), and miscellaneous textile articles ($21 billion).

There's a notion that engaging China in multiple prolonged conflicts could deplete their resources and redirect the focus of the Chinese administration. Additionally, in 2010, China became the world's second-largest economy, surpassing Japan.

The disputed Nine-dash line is China's claim that encircles up to 90% of the contested waters, stretching about 2,000km from the Chinese mainland to within a few hundred kilometers of the Philippines, Malaysia, and Vietnam. The Philippines is contesting these claims at the Permanent Court of Arbitration in The Hague, seeking clarification on disputed areas as islands, low-tide coral outcrops, or submerged banks to define territorial waters as per the convention.

The origin of the line traces back to its appearance as an 11-dash line on a Chinese map in 1947. At that time, the Republic of China's navy took control of islands in the South China Sea previously occupied by Japan during World War II. Beijing further solidified its presence in the northern part of these waters in the mid-1970s, particularly by expelling the South Vietnamese navy from the Paracel Islands, resulting in a fatal clash.

Over subsequent decades, China gained control over seven reefs in the Spratly Islands during the 1980s and 1990s, with the Scarborough Shoal coming under Chinese control in 2012. Taiwan continues to assert its maritime claims in the region, maintaining a military garrison on Pratas Islands and the largest natural feature in the Spratlys, Taiping.

The significance of the line lies in its foundation for China's claim to "historical rights" within the region, encompassing more than 2 million square kilometers. This claim contrasts with other claimants, such as the Philippines, Malaysia, and Brunei, whose assertions are based on geographical proximity, while Vietnam emphasizes active administration over the largest number of islands and reefs in the Spratlys.

China's strategy with the nine-dash line is deliberately ambiguous. While a signatory to UNCLOS, Beijing has deliberately refrained from defining the legal meaning of the line, leaving room for interpretation. This ambiguity fosters multiple interpretations—some believe it denotes China's maritime boundary, while others assert it delineates areas China aims to control rather than the waters themselves.

China's lack of precise articulation regarding the nine-dash line in the South China Sea allows for diverse interpretations, facilitating possible over-interpretation and actions that respond to perceived encroachments within the demarcated area.

The dispute between Japan and China over the Senkaku Islands stems from historical agreements. The Senkaku Islands were included in the 1972 Okinawa Reversion Agreement between the United States and Japan, indicating their consistent inclusion as part of Japanese territory in the post-war international order and in compliance with international law.

In China, the establishment of the infrastructure ecosystem spanned over 30 years. A proposed goal involves obtaining control over the infrastructure and manufacturing ecosystem within this sphere.

## -How china is controlling the African countries-

China has played a significant role in developing Nigeria's infrastructure, focusing on areas like railroads, electricity, ICT, and oil refineries due to Nigeria's substantial oil reserves. Over 20 companies are involved in these ventures.

Additionally, China has flooded Nigeria with inexpensive Chinese goods, as reported by The New York Times, impacting the local market.

The Straits of Malacca, a critical global shipping route, connect the Indian Ocean to the Pacific Ocean, facilitating trade among major economies such as the Middle East, China, Japan, and South Korea. With over 200 vessels passing through daily, this route transports 80% of oil to Northeast Asia and one-third of the world's traded goods, including Chinese products and Indonesian coffee. The straits, linking over 700 ports, serve as a vital trade chokepoint.

The Andaman and Nicobar Command (ANC) represent the sole tri-service theatre command of the Indian Armed Forces active in the Andaman-Nicobar region. Blocking the Malacca Strait by the Indian Navy would severely impact China, prompting vigorous efforts by China to regain control of the strait from the Indian military.

The Straits of Malacca, stretching 550 miles between Sumatra's east coast and the Malay Peninsula's west coast, witness the passage of over 70,000 ships annually. This waterway is pivotal for global trade due to its significance in transporting roughly a quarter of the world's sea-based oil, more than 15 million barrels daily, upon which several countries, including China and Japan, heavily rely.

This chokepoint can significantly impact the global economy and manufacturing centers worldwide. It possesses the potential to restrain China's energy imports and limit its exports to other regions. India could potentially restrict China's 80% oil imports from the Middle East by blocking access to the Malacca Strait, a move that might compel China to seek aalternative oil import routes, such as Pakistan's CPEC and Gwadar extending to the Arctic Circle.

# -Teams for WORLD WAR 3<sup>RD</sup>-

| US + Allies | Eastern powers |
|---|---|
| US + Japan + Britain + India + Taiwan + France + Ukraine + South Korea + Belarus | Russia + China + North Korea + Pakistan + Iran. |

# -MAJOR EVENTS TIME LINE-

| sl | DATE | EVENT |
|---|---|---|
| 1 | NOV 2023 | • Fed new rate hike practically effect the market. |
| 2 | JAN 2024 | • Europe will be in official recession. |
| 3 | JAN 2024 | • Taiwan's President Election – very important event for China. |
| 4 | JAN 2024 | • BRICS new members- Argentina, Egypt, Ethiopia, Iran, Saudi Arabia, and the United Arab Emirates…………effecting. |
| 5 | MAR 2024 | • Interest rate cut by the U.S Fed<br>• Financial reprecession starts after the new decresed interest rate affects market. |
| 6 | JUNE 2024 | • Prime Minister Election in India – MODI – 3<sup>rd</sup> term starts. |
| 7 | JULY 2024 | • U. S - Regional banks will start collapsing – Bail In. |
| 8 | NOV 2024 | • Election of the U.S President. |
| 9 | 2025 | • US - One by one all small – medium & regional banks will be engulfed by FED. Bank consolidation. |
| 10 | 2025 | • Engage Russia in kinetic war in Baltic Sea region. |
| 11 | 2025 | • China actively invade Taiwan. Official start of WW 3. |
| 12 | 2026 JAN | • CBCD AND DIGITAL ID will be implemented in U.S and India. |

| 13 | 2028 | • North Korea invade South Korea. |
|---|---|---|
| 14 | 2028 | • Japan invade China. |
| 15 | 2028 | • Russia directly confronts NATO in Europe. Europe will be big battle ground. |
| 16 | 2029 | • U.S and India will be cash less economy. |
| 17 | 2029 | • Regime change in India, MODI govt topple down.<br>• New weak PM with weak cabinet ministry for India. |
| 18 | 2030 | • Indo –Pakistan kinetic war starts – long time line at least for 8 months. |
| 19 | 2030 | • We need some constitutional changes in India. So, we can control the puppet govt longer time. |
| 20 | 2030 | • Indo – China kinetic war starts – long time line at least for 2 years. |
| 21 | 2032 | • Full economic colonization after the end of the war, new world order under the rule of "One world Government". |

# -THE END-